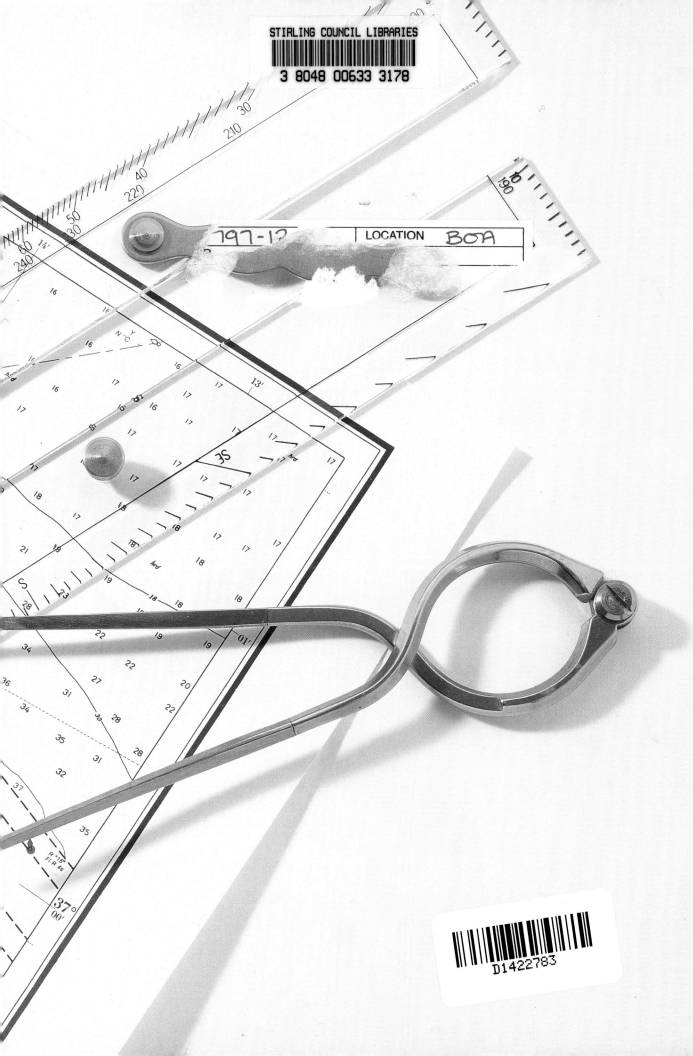

The SAILING
H A N D B O O K

The
SAILING
H A N D B O O K

Dave Cox

NH
NEW
HOLLAND

First published in 1999 by
New Holland Publishers Ltd
London • Cape Town • Sydney • Auckland

24 Nutford Place
London W1H 6DQ
United Kingdom

80 McKenzie Street
Cape Town 8001
South Africa

14 Aquatic Drive
Frenchs Forest, NSW 2086
Australia

218 Lake Road
Northcote, Auckland
New Zealand

ISBN 1 85368 780 4 (hard cover)
ISBN 1 85368 793 6 (soft cover)

Publishing Manager: Mariëlle Renssen
Senior Designer: Lyndall du Toit
Editors: Thea Grobbelaar, Mariëlle Renssen
Illustrator: Steven Felmore
Consultants: James Jermain (UK),
  Jeff Toghill (Australia)
Picture Researcher: Carmen Watts
Reproduction by Unifoto (Pty) Ltd
Printed and bound in Singapore by Tien Wah Press
  (Pte) Ltd
10 9 8 7 6 5 4 3 2 1

Publisher's acknowledgements
The Publishers would like to extend their heartfelt thanks
to the following people for their assistance and expertise:
Dr Peter Goldman for going the extra mile to research
information, photograph specific requests and delve into
his extensive photographic library for us; Central Boating
for lending us their equipment as props; and Keith Moir at
the Weather Bureau and Dr Wayne Smith at Emergency
Medical Services for their advice and verification of facts.

*Although the author and publishers have made every effort
to ensure that the information contained in this book was
correct at the time of going to press, they accept no
responsibility for any loss, injury or inconvenience
sustained by any person using this book.*

CONTENTS

CHAPTER ONE

A HISTORICAL OVERVIEW

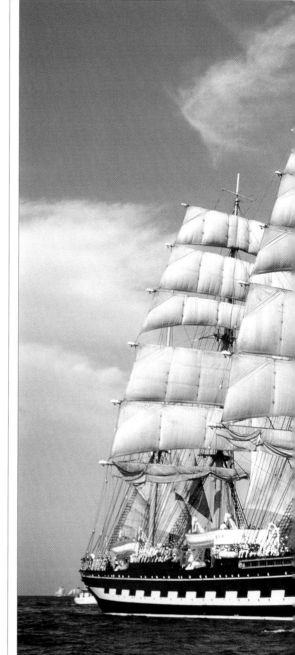

Top *A lateen-sailed dhow, still used today by the Arabs.*
Above *The standing and running rigging of an old square-rigged sailing ship.*

Boats have been in evidence from very early times in the history of man on earth. Perhaps thousands of years ago man discovered that a sail of some sort would carry him downwind without him having to work at his paddles or oars, and the first sailing boats were conceived. However, the research that has been recorded on man's maritime heritage, and the many books that have been written, are mostly confined to a specific niche in the history of boats and ships. In this chapter the general development of vessels propelled by sail is briefly discussed.

Most laymen understand that boats can be driven downwind – that is, with the wind – like a leaf blown by a breeze. Going upwind, or to windward (against the wind), is more complex, and perhaps something of a mystery to those not familiar with sailing. So it was with early sailing vessels; they were built to go downwind. Only later were the possibilities of going to windward appreciated. This ability was then steadily developed over centuries. Early ships, particularly those of the 15th-century Spanish and Portuguese seafaring explorers, were for the most part square-rigged (*see* illustration, page 12), that is,

the bulk of the sails were rectangular in shape, set ahead of the masts at right angles to the length of the ship and supported at the top by yards. Most square-rigged ships could sail not only directly downwind, but across the wind and all angles in between. As the design evolved, square-rigged ships, with their yards (spars from which the sails were hung) trimmed as close to the centre line as pos-

The Russian square-rigged tall ship Kruzenshtern.

Below *A Chinese junk, characterized by its aft high freeboard (the deck's height above the water) and its battened sails.*

Below *This Viking craft, derived from the dugout (records of a fully developed vessel date back to 300BC), was sailed by early Scandinavian seafarers. Its single square sail could be manipulated to enable the vessel to sail with the wind at right angles to the vessel.*

sible, could even make 'ground to windward' (sail into the wind). This, however, was never the square-rig's forte and as the world was opened up by early European explorers, the trade routes that were developed followed the established weather systems of the world to enable ships to sail downwind for the majority of their voyage. While those with their roots in Europe concentrated on the square-riggers,

different sailing craft were developing in other parts of the world. The Polynesians travelled the vast Pacific in fast, frail, multihull vessels based on canoes. Arabs developed the famous dhows, with their lateen rigs, which traded regularly across the Indian Ocean, and the Chinese sailed their junks. In the Mediterranean, feluccas and other craft developed. Many of these

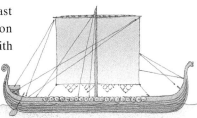

were fore-and-aft rigged, rather than square-rigged – a breakthrough for sailing upwind. This rig in its various forms comprised headsails usually set ahead of the mainmast, with the mainsail set behind the mainmast, attached by its leading edge (luff) to the mast.

Early fore-and-aft rigged boats were often gaff-rigged – that is, the mainsail, and the mizzen (the aftermost fore-and-aft sail) in the case of ketches and yawls, was four-sided, with the top supported by a spar, or gaff (*see* illustrations).

The square-rig continued well into the 20th century as it was suitable (because of its size) for driving clippers and commercial sailing ships carrying general cargo, grain and coal. However, for fishing fleets, pilot vessels and fast naval vessels used for scouting and communication, the square-rig was not versatile enough or good enough at going to windward. From these fleets developed many different types of fore-and-aft rigged vessels, each ideally suited to its specific environment. Pilot cutters had to be able to stay at sea in all weather. So did many of the fishing fleets. Some had to go to windward to reach or return from their fishing grounds or pilot stations.

Many of the early pleasure yachts were descended directly from these working craft. Particularly in the first 50 years of this century, those yachts used for round-the-world voyages were converted from fore-and-aft working vessels, or built along their lines.

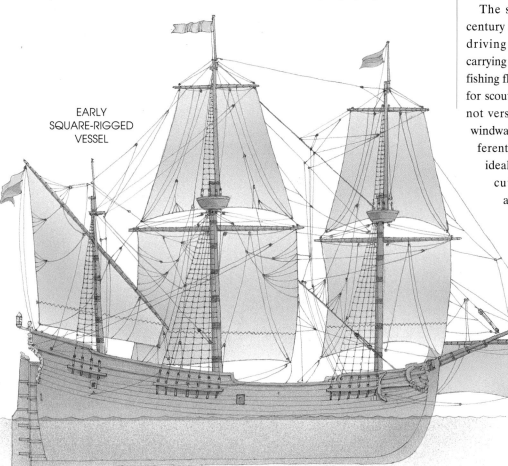

EARLY SQUARE-RIGGED VESSEL

SAILING FOR PLEASURE

When did man start sailing for pleasure? In earlier days, square-rigged naval vessels carried many small craft on deck, all of which could be rowed, while some could be sailed; officers must have sailed them for pleasure. They certainly did in more modern times, when World War I and II warships carried double-ended boats of the 'naval whaler' type. These whalers were used for training as well as racing.

Fishing fleets and pilot boats often organized annual race days for their working craft. Many pictures originating in the 1800s remain to this day, showing such craft on their annual race. In Sydney Harbour, open sailing boats were used to attend the square-riggers anchored in the harbour. They too were raced by their professional crews, and it was from them that the famous Sydney Harbour 18ft Skiff Class evolved.

GAFF-RIGGED VESSEL

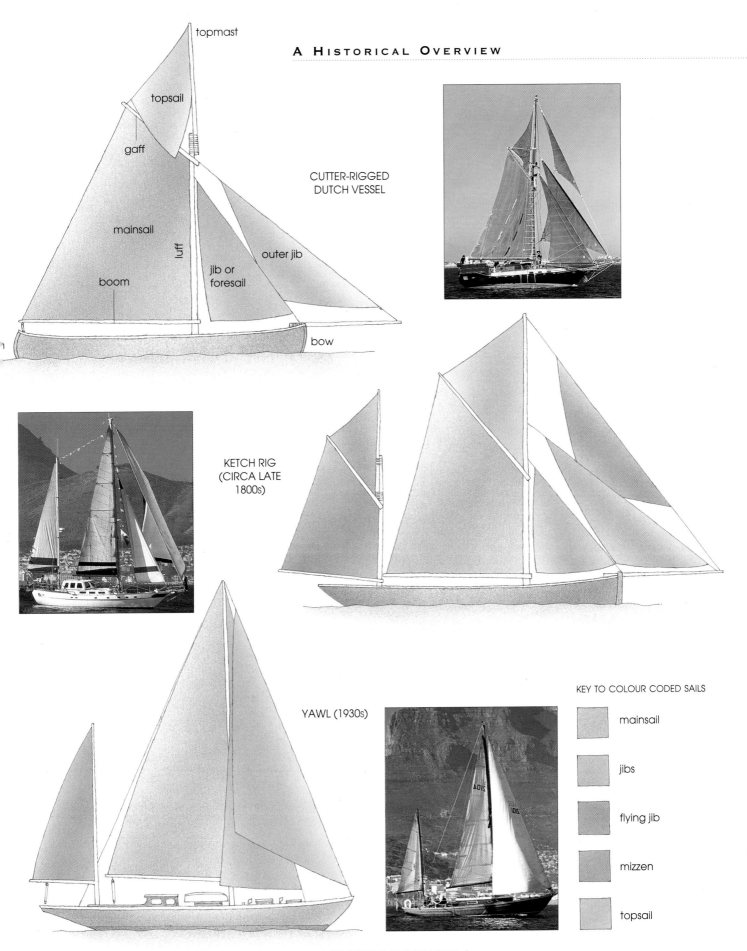

topmast

topsail

gaff

mainsail

luff

outer jib

jib or foresail

boom

bow

CUTTER-RIGGED
DUTCH VESSEL

KETCH RIG
(CIRCA LATE
1800s)

YAWL (1930s)

KEY TO COLOUR CODED SAILS

mainsail

jibs

flying jib

mizzen

topsail

EARLY SAILING VESSELS

Yachting's Origins

It appears that the term 'yacht' originated in Holland. The word as it is spelt today is derived from the Dutch *jaght* (later *jacht*), which in the words *jachthond* (hunting hound) and *jachthoren* (hunting horn) has a hunting connotation. However, a *jaghtschip* ('ship for chasing') refers to a swift, light vessel of war.

The Dutch produced many excellent marine artists, of whom two of the most famous were Willem van de Velder the Elder (1611–93) and Willem van de Velder the Younger (1633–1707). They have both captured early yachts on canvas, giving us an excellent idea of what these craft were like. The early pleasure craft resembled smaller versions of naval vessels of the time and were large by today's standards.

In the 17th century young Prince Charles of England (later Charles II) spent some years in exile in Holland. When he was eventually allowed to return to England, the Dutch presented him with a yacht, the *Mary*, as a farewell gift. His period of exile, many believe, resulted in the introduction of yachting into England.

Wealthy men started to own pleasure craft in the 18th century. Regardless of rig, they were all known as yachts. They were initially used for waterborne ceremonies, attended by great pomp. In 1775 the Cumberland Fleet was founded in England; it could well have been the first yacht club in that country. By the close of the 18th century, the Cumberland Fleet had organized racing on the River Thames.

Yachting existed well before this in Cork Harbour, Ireland, and was mentioned as early as 1720. Apparently the Cork Water Club, now the Royal Cork Yacht Club, was already in existence by then.

While yachting appears to have originated in Europe, much subsequent development occurred on the east coast of America. Americans had the reputation of developing some very speedy craft indeed. Some of the fastest clipper ships of the mid-19th century were designed and built by the legendary Donald McKay, who was based in Boston. Records set by McKay's clippers were held for many years.

Fore-and-aft rigged vessels also developed in America. As in Europe, most had their origins in working activities: oyster dredging, fishing (both coastal and on the Grand Banks), and pilot work.

Schooner Rigs This was a favourite of the Americans and many beautiful schooners appeared (*see* illustration, left). The boats produced in Great Britain and the USA started to diverge from one another, something apparent until fairly recent times. British yachts tended to be heavy, fairly narrow and deep drafted, sometimes carrying a lot of ballast (iron or lead to increase stability and ensure self-righting), while American boats were often beamier (wider) and shallower with schooner rigs.

This development was really brought home to the British in the mid-1800s when a syndicate of American yachtsmen had the schooner *America* designed and built. She was sailed to England in 1851, where she won a Victorian Cup in a race sailed round the Isle of Wight. She was so far ahead that when Queen Victoria, who watched the finish of the race, asked who was second, the queen was told there was no second! The owners of *America* had hoped to race her in Great Britain for wagers, but after this victory there were no takers. *America* sailed home bearing their Victorian Cup, which later became famous as the America's Cup (*see* panel) and is contested – at the cost of millions of dollars to challengers and defenders alike – to this day.

Bermuda Rigs As discussed earlier, the earlier fore-and-aft rigs were mostly gaff rigs. However, modern development has seen the almost universal acceptance of the Bermuda, or Marconi, rig – today's familiar triangular mainsail. The Bermuda rig has the advantage of being able to point closer to the wind than the gaff rig (that is, the performance to windward is improved). It has disadvantages as well – one is the longer mast required – but these are outweighed by the benefits. There is still a place for the gaff rig (and many of these old boats have survived), but nowadays most boats are designed with the Bermuda rig.

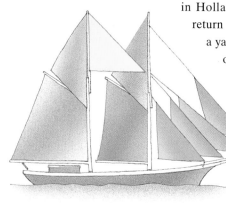

SCHOONER-RIGGED VESSEL (1800s)

Gaff schooner rigs.

BERMUDA-RIGGED KETCH (CIRCA 1920)

THE AMERICA'S CUP

The schooner *America* crossed the North Atlantic from her native America in 1851, to race against British yachts. In her first race at Cowes, where she was pitted against 16 British boats, she won by a considerable margin. The prize was a large Victorian cup which was later named the 'America's Cup' after the famous schooner. The owners had hoped to challenge Britain again that year, but after her runaway victory, no-one would take them on.

In 1857 the original New York syndicate who owned the *America* gave the cup to the New York Yacht Club, on the condition that foreign yachts would be allowed to challenge for it. Race rules stipulated that only two boats were permitted to enter the challenge; the yachts concerned were very large by today's standards, and were usually owned by very rich individuals who came from well-known families, or who had made their money in industry or business.

For many years, the challengers in this prestigious race came only from Great Britain. Initially, until the rules were changed in the 1950s, it was up to the challenger to sail across the Atlantic, while the defender had no such arduous voyage to undertake. Although the British came very close to taking the cup on one or two occasions, they never quite succeeded. Tremendously colourful characters were involved in these titanic battles, among them, on the British side, Sir Thomas Sopwith of aviation fame, and the renowned tea magnate, Sir Thomas Lipton. On the American side were the well-known Vanderbilt family and designers such as Herroshoff, Burgess and Stephens.

In the final years before World War II, the famous J Class of boat evolved for the race. Their price makes them totally unsuitable for today's world, but they were truly magnificent in their day and several are still sailing.

After World War II there were no more challengers until the deeds of the cup were rewritten, making the much smaller 12-metre Class the boat for the America's Cup. Starting in the late 1950s, a series of challenges by British 12-metre boats was successfully defended by the Americans.

By this stage other nations had also become interested, and the rules were changed to allow a number of challengers to engage in a series of races to select the best challenger, who would then meet the American defender. These preliminary races were held in Newport, Rhode Island, USA until 1987.

Over the years, Britain, France, Italy, Sweden, and Australia sent 12-metre boats to challenge the Americans, but until 1983 the Americans managed to win the best of nine series and retain the cup. In 1983, however, the challenge led by Australian Allan Bond was successful. The *Australia III*, designed by Ben Lexcen, financed by Allan Bond, and sailed by skipper John Bertrand and his team, put up a nail-biting performance, and only clinched the series by winning the last race, beating America's Dennis Conner. The next cup event was held off Fremantle, Australia, in 1986, where Dennis Conner reclaimed the cup.

The New Zealanders were the next challengers. At this event, held off San Diego on the west coast of the USA in 1989, a catamaran sailed by Dennis Conner beat a giant monohull from New Zealand. It was a total mismatch and was the subject of a number of court cases which threatened to end the America's Cup. The debacle resulted in a new set of rules which produced a new class of yachts for the race. The last event, sailed in 1995 off San Diego, was won by New Zealander Russell Coutts and his team. The next event is scheduled for the year 2000 and will be held off Auckland, New Zealand.

Dennis Conner, based in San Diego, has been at the pinnacle of competitive sailing for some three decades. Initially an amateur sailor, he soon turned professional as his involvement increased. His career has encompassed all facets of sailing, from dinghies through keelboats and offshore racers to the major races.

During the time that the Southern Ocean Racing Circuit (SORC) – held in winter in the waters off Florida – was attaining its peak, it served as the breeding ground for the American teams to the Admiral's Cup. Dennis Conner was usually there. He was always a top contender, and often won overall.

His name is synonymous with the America's Cup – his outspoken comments in this arena have not always been tactful, earning him the nickname of 'big bad Dennis': the sailor that sailors love to hate.

In 1983 he was the first American to lose the America's Cup – to the Australians. However, Conner bounced right back and recaptured the cup in

1986. He and his team won again in the controversial race of 1989, sailing their catamaran against the New Zealand monohull. In 1995, Conner lost the cup once more, this time to the New Zealanders while sailing off San Diego. No doubt he will be at the America's Cup in 2000.

Conner sails smaller boats as well, and usually turns up for the World Championship of the Etchells 22 Class, a 22ft (6,5m) three-man keelboat. Needless to say he has won this championship a number of times. During the Toshiba Challenge in the Whitbread Round-the-World Race in 1997/98, although he only sailed some of the legs, he is credited with raising the money and generally putting the campaign together.

Despite the fact that Dennis Conner will always be known as 'Mr America's Cup', his credits include winning the SORC four times and the world championships in the Star and Etchells 22 classes, and receiving a bronze medal in the Olympic Games held in 1976.

Above *Boats of the Sigma 33 One Design fleet racing in the UK.*

Right *The boat type (Europe Dinghy Class) illustrated here is used in the Women's Olympic single- handed dinghy class.*

Yacht Racing

Yacht racing was well established by the mid-1800s. It was a problem, however, that races generally tended to be won by the largest boats, supported by the mathematical formula that relates the maximum speed of a displacement hull (one that is not planing) to its waterline length. The longer the waterline, the faster the potential top speed of the craft. This is simplistic, as other factors such as beam, displacement and sail area are involved. Nonetheless, it is normally accepted that the longer the craft, the faster it is able to sail.

This resulted in the need for a method of handicapping, or rating the craft. It is one of the most difficult aspects in the racing of dissimilar craft and has resulted in many different rating rules over the past 150 years, not one of which has been perfect. The main problem seems to be that no matter how careful or thorough the authors of the rules are, the competitive designers, owners and crew tend to find loopholes in them. Designs are then aimed at exploiting the loopholes and the rules inadvertently favour certain types of boats.

The characteristics a craft requires to rate well under a rule are not always desirable ones and can adversely affect seaworthiness, steering ability and stability. The simple rules of 100 years ago cannot stand the pressure brought to bear by today's designers and sailors, who now have immense computer power at their disposal. The problem of fairly rating dissimilar yachts is one that may never be solved in an entirely satisfactory manner.

Complicating the matter even further in earlier times was the fact that different rating rules developed on different sides of the Atlantic. This made it difficult for European and American yachts to compete with each other on a fair basis. Only in 1970 did the International Offshore Rule (IOR) come into universal use, binding international competition to the same rule. It has since been superseded and has been replaced by International Measurement System (IMS), itself under pressure to survive at the top level of international racing.

To avoid the complications of rating rules, racing under the Performance Handicap Racing Fleet (PHRF) system is popular in some parts of the world. PHRF is not properly scientific as it judges a boat's potential over a number of races, altering a craft's PHRF factor as performance improves or decreases. Perhaps you can liken it to the golf handicap system, but it provides many club level sailors with an acceptable formula under which to race.

One-designs Many sailors did not want to be bothered with handicap rules so this century saw the development of several one-design classes, mainly at the bottom size range of the fleets. The principle of a one-design class is that all boats are essentially equal. Crews then compete on equal terms and theoretically the best crew wins. The bulk of the one-design classes originated in Europe, the UK and the USA. Some have become international and some have endured for 80 years or more.

One disadvantage of the one-design concept is that development is restricted, if not eliminated, by the class rules. If all racing were done in one-designs, the spectacular developments that have taken place in yacht design and construction would probably not have occurred.

The Sailing Explosion

Until this century, much of the sailing described so far was the preserve of the rich, who had their craft maintained and sailed by professional crews. The huge increase in small-boat sailing occurred this century, with the sport becoming accessible to a wider public. Many of the early one-designs were small half-decked keelboats sailed by crews of about three, while others were dinghies. These classes attracted newcomers. They were cheaper, did not require large crews, and could be sailed by most people. For instance, the 15ft (4.5m) Snipe Class of two-man dinghy was designed in the USA in the early 1930s. It is still strong there and has fleets in other parts of the world. The two-man Star Class keelboat also originated in the USA (around the turn of the century). Kept up to date by rule changes, mainly to the rig, the Star is still an international class and has often been used in the Olympic Games.

International Dinghy Racing

In the UK, many local classes existed before World War II, but national sailing took place in the International 14 and National 12 classes. These were restricted classes, different designs being allowed within a set of clear parameters. They were, as their names suggest, 14ft (4.2m) and 12ft (3.6m) long.

What really put a spark into dinghy sailing was the breakthrough that led to the 'planing' dinghy. Many bigger keelboats are known as displacement sailing boats (if they weigh 5 tons, that is how much water they displace). They never rise in the water or

UFFA FOX

Uffa Fox is regarded as the father of the planing dinghy, which he developed in the 1930s, producing a number of highly successful International 14 dinghies.

He was born in 1898 on the Isle of Wight. His parents must have foreseen his boating future when they named him Uffa after the old Norse sea king. He grew up at Cowes, for many years the sailing centre of Great Britain.

Fox's ambition was to become a naval architect, and he took an apprenticeship with S G Saunders, studying boat building and design. At the age of 21, helped by his father, he set up his own business. He believed that if a sailing dinghy were made the right shape and was light enough, it could plane, reducing its effective displacement (weight) and dramatically increasing speed. In her first season the International 14 *Avenger*, one of his early 1930s planing dinghies, took an astounding 52 firsts in 57 starts. For a number of years Fox crewed for Britain's Prince Philip during Cowes Week. He continued designing and sailing boats well into old age. He died in 1972.

One of his designs was the airborne lifeboat, streamlined to facilitate being attached to an aircraft. Parachuted down to ditched World War II airmen, these boats saved many lives. They were sought-after even in peacetime and many were converted to cruising sailboats.

Perhaps the best known of Uffa Fox's designs is the Flying Fifteen, a fin-keeler.

Flying Fifteens being sailed at Cowes Week.

lift up like a speedboat, thereby reducing their displacement and wetted surface. They are limited to a speed of around 1.4 multiplied by the square root of LWL (the Length of the Waterline). Planing removes this speed limit.

The first American scows, flattish boats with a rounded or spoon bow, planed. Early in the 1900s, a class of 25ft (7.6m) and 20ft (6.1m) scows in South Africa – based on the American ones – planed at high speeds. Whether or not the designers of these scows achieved this by design, or hit upon the right shape purely by accident, is not known.

Above *An International 14 dinghy planing, with both sailors out on the trapeze.*

Post World War II

The sailing explosion really got under way after World War II, when sailing took a decisive move away from being a sport for the wealthy. One of the reasons for this was plywood sailing dinghies that could be built at home. Monthly yachting magazines or, in some cases, newspapers promoted designs or classes – and their popularity was assured.

Some of these, for instance, the Enterprise Class, the Mirror Dinghy and the Fireball Class, are still popular but because lifestyles and building materials have changed, not many are built at home these days. The one-design rules have been modified regularly to allow building in glass fibre, resulting in modern, low-maintenance construction for the same weight and, theoretically, the same performance.

From the large group of people who started sailing these dinghies, many eventually moved to day-racing keelboats and offshore racers, giving a big fillip to this level of sailing too. With travel becoming easier, it became commonplace for international competitors to take part in events around the world. In addition, many of the one-design dinghy classes moved their championships to various different countries.

In the UK, the well-known designer Uffa Fox (*see* panel, page 17) researched and developed planing. He raced International 14s in the 1930s and when he produced the first 14s capable of planing, the rest were outclassed. It is from his trend-setting design that most of today's high-performance sailing dinghies have evolved. Boats have also become lighter through the low weights achieved by today's hi-tech building materials. They are therefore able to plane much faster in much less wind, and many are capable of planing to windward.

Ocean Voyaging

Ocean voyaging for pleasure, a completely different sector of the many-faceted sport of sailing, developed at the turn of the century. The first known round-the-world yacht circumnavigation was that done by Captain Joshua Slocum (*see* panel, opposite) in 1895 in his 36ft (10.9m) sloop/yawl, *Spray* (the yacht commenced her circumnavigation as a sloop and ended it as a yawl, after changes made by her redoubtable skipper). Captain Slocum was a master mariner and knew the oceans of the world. His was a true pioneering voyage and it set standards and opened doors for others to follow – several notable ocean passages took place between the conclusion of Slocum's voyage and the commencement of World War II.

A TYPICAL SAILING DINGHY

It was also only after the war that the trade-wind routes began to be populated by yachts embarking on ocean voyages. It was much easier than in Slocum's day because the opening of the Panama Canal meant that sailing yachts could take the short cut from the Atlantic Ocean to the Pacific (or vice versa), without having to round Cape Horn or go through the Straits of Magellan.

Helping to popularize ocean voyaging was a quiet, unassuming British couple, Susan and Eric Hiscock (*see* panel, page 119). Not only were the Hiscocks superb amateur sailors, Eric was also an excellent writer and photographer. His work helped to educate the sailing public on how to make sailing voyages skilfully and safely, and also on how to behave in foreign ports where different customs prevailed. Nowadays, thanks to all the literature produced on long-distance voyaging, it is much easier to sail across the oceans.

Offshore and Ocean Racing

While interest in dinghy sailing increased, and more and more sailors explored the oceans, offshore and ocean racing was developing apace. The 650-nautical-mile Fastnet Race (from Cowes to Plymouth via the Fastnet Rock off the coast of Ireland) was first sailed in 1925.

JOSHUA SLOCUM

Joshua Slocum was a professional sea captain who earned his place in yachting history by being the first person to circumnavigate the world in a yacht – an outstanding feat that was achieved single-handed.

Born in Wilmot, Nova Scotia, Canada, in 1846, Joshua Slocum went to sea at the tender age of 16. All his voyages were to foreign parts. Over the passing years, he became a professional captain and owned shares in some of the craft he sailed. One of them, the *Aquidneck*, was unfortunately wrecked in 1885 near Montevideo. No lives were lost, but Slocum had to find a way of getting himself, and his family who were with him, back to the USA. With the meagre tools available to him, he built the 35ft (10.6m) *Liberdade*. According to Slocum, the hull was a cross between a Cape Ann dory and a sampan; she was also junk-rigged. In the *Liberdade*, crewed by his family, he completed a voyage of 5500 miles (8700km), returning to the USA in 1888. Slocum's most famous small-boat voyage was to follow. He was presented with an old wreck which he rebuilt, and *Spray* was the result. On 24 April 1895, aided by *Spray*'s unusual ability to steer herself, he sailed single-handedly from Boston, returning three years and two months later (17 June 1898) to drop anchor at Newport. Although self-steering gear is common today, it was unknown at that time. Because the Panama Canal was not open then, Slocum either had to round the notorious Cape Horn or sail through the Straits of Magellan; he chose the latter.

In the years since Slocum's historic voyage, many *Spray* replicas have been built, and several have made long and successful ocean passages. Slocum's book, *Sailing Around the World*, is still obtainable and is well worth reading, even a hundred years later.

In 1905, 1907 and 1908, Slocum single-handedly undertook winter cruises aboard *Spray* to the West Indies. In 1909, after fitting out at the famous Herreshoff boatworks, Slocum (63 years old at the time) set off on his normal voyage south aboard *Spray*. He and his boat disappeared without a trace and no wreckage was ever found.

A gaff-rigged Dixi-Rollar design, based on Slocum's Spray.

Above *Entrants in the Sydney to Hobart Classic yacht race, held on 26 December.*

Right *Whitbread 60s: up-to-date hi-tech ocean racing boats.*

The Bermuda Race – from Newport, Rhode Island, in the USA to Bermuda in the North Atlantic – was inaugurated as far back as 1906, although it lapsed for some years thereafter. Both these races are now sailed biennially. The Australian Sydney to Hobart Classic was initiated in 1945 on Boxing Day (26 December) and is sailed annually.

Longer races, such as the Transpac, from Los Angeles, USA, to Hawaii in the Pacific; the Cape to Rio from South Africa to Brazil, South America; and the Transatlantic Single-Handed Race from England to the USA, have become established over the last 40 years or so. Two of the more spectacular races are the Whitbread Round-the-World Race (now renamed, *see* page 22) for fully crewed boats, and the Around Alone single-handed round-the-world race. Apart from circumnavigating the world, the difference between these and the more conventional transoceanic races is that they take the yachts deep into the Southern Ocean. Here they encounter the Roaring Forties and Screaming Fifties, and, in the extreme southern limits of the course, the danger of collisions with icebergs and growlers. The BT (British Telecom) Challenge tests sailors to the extreme, forcing them to sail around the world against, rather than with, the wind.

WHITBREAD ROUND-THE-WORLD RACE

Towards the end of 1973, the first Whitbread Round-the-World Race started in Portsmouth, England. It was a very different race from the Whitbread of today as, at the time, not many of the yachtsmen were professionals. The race was made up of well-known sailing personalities who on the whole had taken time off from their careers. Many were underfunded and had to raise their own finance in order to compete. The back-up shore teams each competitor has today were also unknown then.

What made them do it? It may have been the challenge of the Southern Ocean, beyond the three fearsome capes – South Africa's Cape of Good Hope (Cape of Storms), Australia's Cape Leeuwin and South America's notorious Cape Horn. It was uncomfortable, dangerous, time-consuming and damaging to careers, and on some boats the crew was required to contribute to expenses.

That first race saw many of the big names of the time competing: Robin Knox-Johnston and Leslie Williams, France's hero Eric Tabarly, British Chay Blyth, and Frenchman André Viant. The best funded, and probably the best organized, was Mexican millionaire Ramon Carlin with his beautiful Swan 65, *Sayula*. Ramon, who had members of his family on board, was not the favourite to win, yet in spite of *Sayula* rolling over off Tasmania, win he did!

The race was sailed every four years thereafter. Ports of call changed from time to time, but the two legs through the Southern Ocean remained, as did the rounding of the three famous capes. With the passing years, the stature of the race increased, boats were designed and built specifically to win it, and sponsors made their appearance, as did the new breed of professional sailors over the past 15 to 20 years. The participation of these professionals projected the Whitbread into ever higher levels of competition, as they now made their living from racing sailboats. As the competition became fiercer, winning times became faster.

Then the special class Whitbread 60 was designed for the race. A number of these superfast boats, about 64ft (19.4m) long, appeared for the 1993/94 race. They were so successful and the racing between them so close, the organizers decided that the 1997/98 race would be restricted to only Whitbread 60s.

Television coverage had also improved and the competing yachts were fitted with equipment which could send TV footage back to base via satellites. Public exposure of the race increased rapidly. Records were broken and the public was treated to spectacular footage of these boats travelling at speeds of up to 30 knots, unheard of for this type of boat until not many years ago.

The much publicized 1997/98 Whitbread event was won by a newcomer to the race, American Paul Cayard, sailing *E.F. Language*. While this was Cayard's first appearance in a long-distance event like the Whitbread, he does hold an impressive record as a professional – he has sailed in and won many world championships, and has competed in both the Admiral's Cup and the America's Cup.

Note: The rights to the Whitbread Round-the-World Race have been bought by the Volvo company, and the race has since been renamed the Volvo Ocean Race. However, the Whitbread 60s will remain the class for the event scheduled in 2001/2002.

These pages *Modern ocean racing in Whitbread 60s.* **Inset** *Skipper Mikaela von Koskull, part of an all-women crew participating in the Whitbread race.*

PROGRESS MADE IN BOAT DESIGN
Monohulled Craft

Changes in the design of sailing dinghies have been discussed earlier, on page 17. Where monohulls (single-hulled vessels) are concerned, design has been revolutionized in the last 50 years. Before this period, most offshore racing yachts and cruisers were heavy and long-keeled, with rudders attached to the end of the keel. As modern glues were devised and construction methods improved, the boats became lighter and designers made them flatter. Fin keels replaced those built into the traditional 'wineglass' hull sections of older boats, and the rudders were separated from the keels, working independently at the aft end of the boat. Wood gave way to fibreglass, with cored fibreglass construction reducing weight even further.

The hi-tech revolution saw top racing boats using carbon fibre, Kevlar (*see* page 59) and special resins in their construction with, as a result, much lighter, even faster boats. The current ocean racer is considerably lighter, much flatter, and has a deep fin keel and a separate rudder. It also has a large sail area which it carries better than its counterpart of 50 years ago. To a lesser extent, the trend is evident in most modern cruising boats as well.

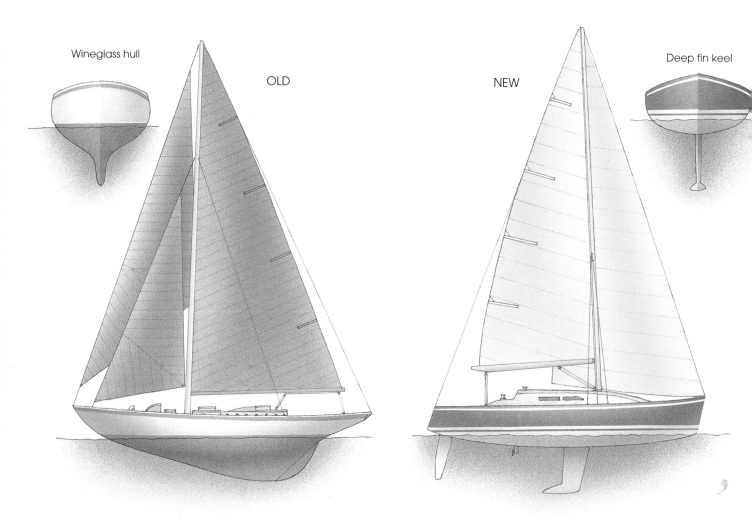

Wineglass hull

OLD

NEW

Deep fin keel

A heavy displacement, long keel ocean racer from the 1930s.

A light displacement offshore racer with separate spade rudder and fin keel.

Multihulled Craft

While the Polynesians and others specialized in multihulled sailing craft hundreds of years ago, the Western world only really accepted them in the last 50 years. Initially, the multihulls were not particularly fast, but in the last 25 years, that has changed. The hi-tech multihulls are extremely fast – indeed, they capture record after record. The Jules Verne Trophy was created for a nonstop voyage around the world in 80 days, and this record has now been smashed by three different multihulled craft: two catamarans (designed with two hulls) and a trimaran (three hulls). However, these hi-tech boats are not for cruising as they can, and do, capsize in spite of the immense size of the bigger ones.

The design of cruising multihulled craft is completely different, and spacious docile craft that are particularly suitable for shallow water sailing areas are now being produced. Many can be beached safely in areas with little or no surf. They are also safe, and adept at crossing oceans – multihulls have ventured into most of the world's great seas.

A TYPICAL SMALL CATAMARAN

Small multihull classes, similar in size to sailing dinghies, have developed apace over the past 40 years. Perhaps the best known of these classes are the Hobie 16 and the Hobie 14. The former is a craft where both the skipper and crew member trapeze (*see* page 103), while the latter is a single-handed craft. Many are sailed at sea after being launched through the surf. Hobies are used for social sailing and serious racing. Together with other designs in the same category, they fill an important role in the small-boat scene.

Left *A Hobie Cat sailing in ideal conditions.*

Following pages *Cowes Week 1998 in the UK.*

CHAPTER TWO

THE NATURAL LAWS OF SAILING

WEATHER

Assuming one has the correct boat, equipment and crew for the type of sailing you want to do, the next most important factor is the weather. The windier conditions are, the more likely it is that you will encounter problems. In the early days of gaining experience, do not go looking for trouble on days when it is blowing a gale. Once you know some of the basic principles of the weather relevant to your area, you can combine your knowledge with the local weather forecast and come to a reasonable conclusion about what to expect on a specific day.

The sun is what makes all forms of life on earth possible. It is also the major factor in creating the weather. Aided by the daily rotation of the earth, and the earth's annual elliptical path around the sun, it is responsible for the wind systems, the currents, the different seasons, the daily variation in weather and, together with the moon, for the tides.

Most areas of the world have definite weather patterns. Some sailing areas have perfect conditions almost on a year-round basis. However, most sailors living in the USA and Europe in the northern hemisphere, or in South America, Southern Africa and Australasia in the southern hemisphere, have to deal with ever-changing weather conditions. The major player is the prevailing westerly airflow in both the northern and southern hemispheres. In the upper atmosphere, this airflow, known as the Westerlies, broadens out, occupying most of the

Above *Caught in heavy wind and wild sea.*

Strong winds in the Algarve, Portugal.

space between the North Pole and the Equator in the northern hemisphere, while in the southern hemisphere the reverse is true.

Weather should be taken seriously by all sailors. If possible, never go to sea without a forecast for the day or, if undertaking a passage, a long-range forecast. Radio and television stations have regular forecasts, and weather offices often have a regularly updated 24-hour phone-in taped service available. Most weather offices will accept a phoned-in enquiry from sailors requiring more detail. Coast radio stations, set up to cater for the radio telephone requirements of ships and small craft, offer forecasts several times a day on nominated radio frequencies. It should not be difficult to get forecasts in coastal waters.

THE WORLD'S SURFACE WIND SYSTEMS

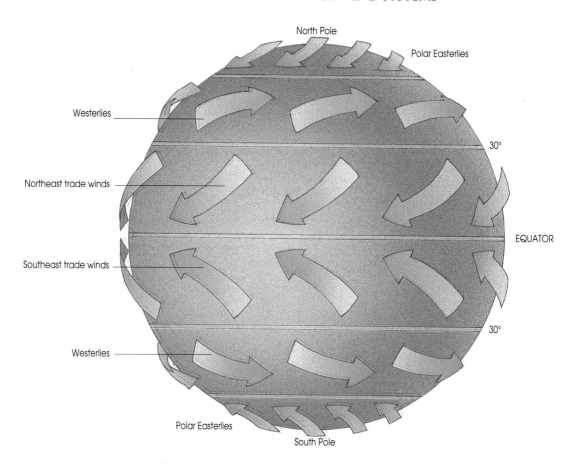

North Pole

Polar Easterlies

Westerlies

30°

Northeast trade winds

EQUATOR

Southeast trade winds

30°

Westerlies

Polar Easterlies

South Pole

A VESSEL'S COURSE AND WIND DIRECTION

An anomaly that once occurred hundreds of years ago is still perpetuated to this day, and could be a trap for the unwary. The course of a vessel always refers to the direction in which she is heading. A vessel on a southerly course is pointing, or heading, south. However, a south wind does not head towards the south, rather, it originates from the south and heads north - the exact opposite of the terms used to describe the vessel's course.

In simple terms, air (wind) flows from areas of high pressure towards areas of low pressure. High pressure areas include the cold polar zones, while areas of very low pressure originate in the tropics (between latitudes 22° north and 22° south). When the barometric pressure (*see* pages 31–32) drops markedly, a change in weather and an increase in wind strength is probably about to occur. The falling barometer will often indicate the approach of a front or low pressure system. (A front is the meeting of two air masses of different origins, for example, the interface of cold polar and warm tropical air, while a low is an area of relatively low atmospheric pressure, e.g. a mid-latitude depression.) Very marked air mass differences, such as tropical meeting polar air, can combine to create severe and sometimes extensive storms. Some storms – cyclones, hurricanes and typhoons – can and do cause considerable damage and loss of life. They are usually picked up well in advance by forecasters, but the problem is that their exact path cannot be forecast accurately. Sailboats should not be at sea in these conditions, if possible.

Many areas have specific weather phenomena. For instance, off the eastern coast of South Africa the 'Westerly Buster' often comes through very suddenly, as does the 'Southerly Buster' off the New South Wales coast in Australia. A marked drop in barometric pressure always precedes these 'Busters'. Get into the habit of watching the barometer and be aware of atmospheric pressure; this is a good guide.

WIND

The illustration above shows the developed surface wind systems of the world. The northeast trade winds in the northern hemisphere and the southeast trades of the southern hemisphere are the primary winds used by today's round-the-world sailors. Before the opening of the Panama Canal, the Westerlies and the trade winds played the most important role in getting commercial sailing ships to their destinations.

Often, in certain areas of the world, when there is no strongly established weather system in place, local factors dictate the wind direction, particularly the land and sea breeze phenomena (*see* illustration right). As these breezes usually blow at right angles to the land, sailboats can reach up and down the shoreline or coast. Even if the winds are light, excellent progress can be made.

Wind strengths that are most suited to a pleasant day's sailing are probably speeds of between 5 and 25 knots (sailing should be a pleasurable activity, after all!). Above 25 knots, the inexperienced can lose control. Already at 18–20 knots dinghies can start planing downwind at high speed, and capsize easily. Both cruisers and ocean racers need to shorten the sail by reefing (taking it in to reduce the surface area) and/or changing down to smaller sails.

Something to keep in mind is the 'weight' of the wind. A 20-knot breeze in squally weather, saturated with moisture at sea, can carry much more clout than the same speed of wind on an inland lake in dry, sunny conditions.

Note: Always have a plan to cope with adverse conditions, which, depending on locality, often come from a similar direction. If the wind drops, accompanied by a dropping barometer, or if there is a radical change in wind direction, or if a bank of dark clouds appears on the horizon, expect a change for the worse. Head for home or shelter until it is clear what the weather has in store. If you suspect the weather may change before starting out, a good plan would be to make sure you are upwind (that is, taking into account the new wind direction) of your home port or club so that you can run back, perhaps with just a jib set. Note, too, that if you are overpowered, you can drop all your sails and quietly take stock of your position.

FORECASTING

In spite of the abundance of scientific equipment available to meteorologists, including the weather satellites orbiting the earth, weather forecasting is not an accurate science. However, accurate weather maps, or synoptic charts (*see* illustration right), can be drawn at a specific moment in time, and many are regularly published. Once you are familiar with weather maps, you can make your own interpretations. A major tool for the sailor is the barometer, which measures atmospheric pressure. The original instrument to measure air pressure was invented in the 17th century by an Italian physicist, Evangelista Torricelli. A column of mercury was contained in a

LAND AND SEA BREEZES

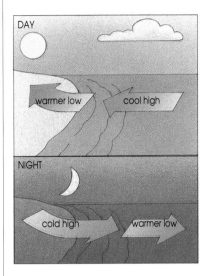

SEA BREEZE The land heats up from the sun, the hot air rises (low pressure area), and a breeze moves in from the colder sea (high pressure area) to replace it.

LAND BREEZE The land cools off, while the sea retains its temperature. The breeze moves from high pressure (land) to lower pressure (sea).

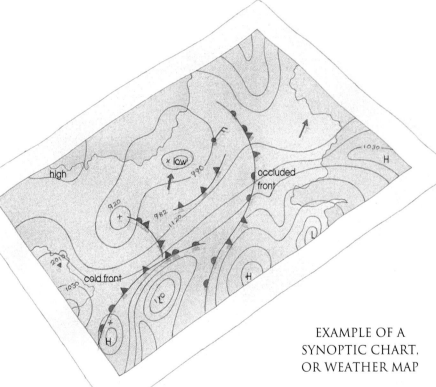

EXAMPLE OF A SYNOPTIC CHART, OR WEATHER MAP

glass tube upended in a dish of mercury. It measured pressure in inches (increased atmospheric pressure on the mercury in the dish pushed the mercury column up the tube), although millibars are the usual measure of pressure today. The pressure seldom dropped below 25.5in (863.5 millibars) or reached a high of

CLOUD FORMATION IN RELATION TO ATMOSPHERIC HEIGHT

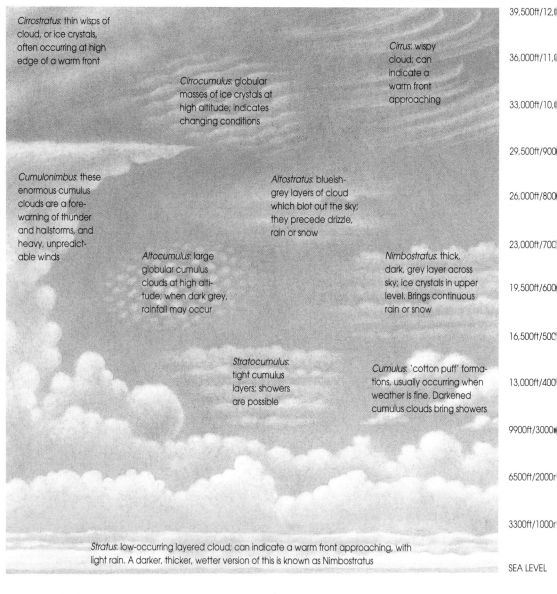

Cirrostratus: thin wisps of cloud, or ice crystals, often occurring at high edge of a warm front

Cirrus: wispy cloud; can indicate a warm front approaching

Cirrocumulus: globular masses of ice crystals at high altitude; indicates changing conditions

Cumulonimbus: these enormous cumulus clouds are a fore-warning of thunder and hailstorms, and heavy, unpredict-able winds

Altostratus: blueish-grey layers of cloud which blot out the sky; they precede drizzle, rain or snow

Altocumulus: large globular cumulus clouds at high alti-tude; when dark grey, rainfall may occur

Nimbostratus: thick, dark, grey layer across sky; ice crystals in upper level. Brings continuous rain or snow

Stratocumulus: tight cumulus layers; showers are possible

Cumulus: 'cotton puff' forma-tions, usually occurring when weather is fine. Darkened cumulus clouds bring showers

Stratus: low-occurring layered cloud; can indicate a warm front approaching, with light rain. A darker, thicker, wetter version of this is known as Nimbostratus

39,500ft/12,0
36,000ft/11,0
33,000ft/10,0
29,500ft/900
26,000ft/800
23,000ft/700
19,500ft/600
16,500ft/500
13,000ft/400
9900ft/3000
6500ft/2000r
3300ft/1000r
SEA LEVEL

CLOUD TYPES

- Alto- = Latin for 'high'
- Cumulus/cumulo- = billowing 'puffy' cloud
- Stratus/strato- = layered cloud
- Nimbus/nimbo- = grey rain cloud
- Cirrus/cirro- = wispy sheets of cloud or contains ice particals

Top *Cirrus cloud;* **centre** *cumulus cloud;* **bottom** *dark, moody clouds indicating that a storm is brewing.* **Right** *Aneroid barometer.* **Following pages** *Close competition at the weather mark during the 1998 Lipton Challenge Cup in Algoa Bay, South Africa.*

some 31.5in (1066.7 millibars). Normal pressure variations are much smaller than this.

This cumbersome instrument was replaced by the aneroid barometer, invented in 1843 by Lucius Vidi. A small, simple instrument, this barometer was robust and lit-tle affected by vessel motion. The navigation station of every seagoing sailboat has one today. It comprises a partially evacuated metal container which expands or contracts as the air pressure decreases or increases. This action is linked to a pointer which indicates the pressure on a clock-like display. A second pointer can be moved by hand to record the existing pressure, and becomes a reference point for any rising/falling pressure there-after. Notations such as 'change', 'fair' or 'rain' print-ed on barometer dials are really too vague to be con-sidered as serious guides to what the weather is going to do. A derivation of the above principle is the baro-graph, which instead of a dial, has a pen that draws an ink line on revolving graph paper, giving a permanent record of pressure and its variation over a period.

TIDES

Tides are different from weather in that they can be forecast with absolute accuracy, and tide tables are published well in advance. They are an invaluable part of any sailor's equipment.

Many of the tidal areas (such as river mouths and lagoons) used by dinghy sailors are inclined to dry out with the receding waters of low tide, leaving sandbanks. A knowledge of tides is essential. The tidal flow in rivers, narrow harbour mouths or passages between islands can also, in some areas, be strong enough to prevent a boat's progress against it.

The gravitational pull of the moon plays the major part in the creation of tides, although it is assisted by the sun (see illustration below). Since the earth completes a full rotation on its axis once every 24 hours and 50 minutes, high water occurs approximately every 12 hours and 25 minutes. The moon in turn orbits the earth in 29.5 days; at full and new moon, both sun and moon are in line with the earth (roughly every fortnight), and we experience spring tides. These are the highest of the high tides and lowest of the low tides, and are caused by the gravitational pull of the moon and the sun working together.

At neap tide, the sun and the moon are at right angles to each other. This occurs during the first and last quarters of the moon. The gravitational forces of the moon and sun are not assisting each other, thus producing the lowest high tides and the highest low tides. This, of course, results in the least movement of water of all the tidal conditions.

In some parts of the world the difference between high and low tide can be negligible or as much as 30ft (9m) or more, so just how much the tide affects you depends on where you do your sailing and on the topography of the area. The enjoyment and safety of the sail may depend very much on getting your tides right – or may be of little consequence.

Note, too, that a strong wind blowing against the tide can produce dangerous waves, as can a strong tide over shoal (shallow) waters.

Several signs indicate which way the tide is flowing, for instance, the wake left by the water movement as it flows past a stake, buoy or headland. And note that away from the centre of a channel or river, the flow lessens considerably, so if you are battling to make progress against a tide, move over to the side. Back eddies at the sides may even assist you, but keep a careful eye on the depth of water.

If you are sailing a keelboat, be especially careful not to run aground on a falling tide. You could be stuck there until the next tide floats you off!

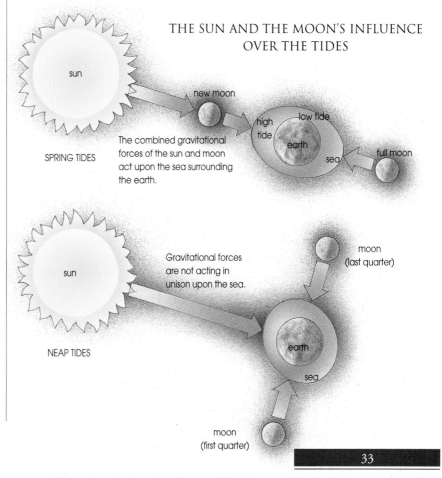

THE SUN AND THE MOON'S INFLUENCE OVER THE TIDES

sun

new moon

high tide

low tide

earth

sea

full moon

SPRING TIDES

The combined gravitational forces of the sun and moon act upon the sea surrounding the earth.

sun

Gravitational forces are not acting in unison upon the sea.

moon (last quarter)

earth

sea

NEAP TIDES

moon (first quarter)

CHAPTER THREE

HOW SAILBOATS WORK

There is much aerodynamic and hydrodynamic theory involved in what makes a sailboat behave as it does. It is easy to understand how a sailboat goes downwind. Just throw a twig or a feather into a pond on a windy day, and it will rapidly move downwind. A sailboat cannot go directly upwind. If you head it into the wind, the sails will flap, the boat will slow down and then move backwards. The nautical term for a boat in this situation is that it is 'in irons'. However, a sailboat can sail some 45 degrees off the true wind, and by making a number of tacks (*see* page 45), it can reach a destination directly upwind of its starting point.

As hull shape influences upwind performance, the hull must be easy to propel through the water. Even more important, it must have good resistance to going sideways (known as leeway), otherwise when the sails are trimmed to go to windward, the boat will not sail forward but rather be blown sideways. This resistance is achieved with a centreboard, or keel.

How Sails Work

Sails are similar in aerofoil shape (*see* page 57) to aircraft and birds' wings, although the sail is a vertical airfoil. The drive to enable a boat to sail upwind is derived in the same manner as the force, or lift,

Above *A crewman making adjustments on the standing rigging of a boat using a bosun's chair.*

which keeps aircraft and birds aloft. When the wind meets the sail surface, it splits: the leeward side acts in a similar way to the top of an aircraft wing as the air, or wind, on this side speeds up and travels faster than that on the windward side of the sail. The pressure is higher on the windward side and this, coupled with low pressure on the leeward side of the sail, results in lift. Provided leeway is largely prev-

Keelboats on the reaching leg of an Olympic-type triangular racing course.

SAILING TERMS

- **Windward**: the direction from which the wind is blowing
- **Leeward**: the direction towards which the wind is blowing
- **Luff up**: to head up vessel into the wind
- **Bear away**: to alter one's course away from the wind
- **Upwind**: a vessel sailing upwind is going to windward
- **Downwind**: sailing with the wind aft of the beam (boat's breadth)
- **True wind**: speed and direction of actual wind as perceived if vessel is stationary
- **Pointing**: heading into the wind
- **Heeling**: leaning over, or listing
- **If wind lifts**: change in wind direction that enables boat to head up on the tack it is undertaking
- **If wind heads**: change in wind direction that forces boat to head lower on the tack it is undertaking

ented, it will drive the boat upwind at an angle of up to 40 degrees to the true wind. You can now execute a series of tacks to reach your upwind destination.

There is no one particular procedure that is perfect – one can devise one's tacks to suit the situation. Navigational hazards may need to be taken into account or the presence of other craft or, when racing is involved, small shifts in wind direction.

Boat Stability

The keel of a boat fulfils two functions: its weight contributes to stability, and the keel itself helps to prevent sideways drift. Few keelboats will fail to right themselves from a 90-degree knock-down position, and ocean-going boats rely on this self-righting ability (many examples exist of seagoing sailing vessels being rolled through 360 degrees – and surviving).

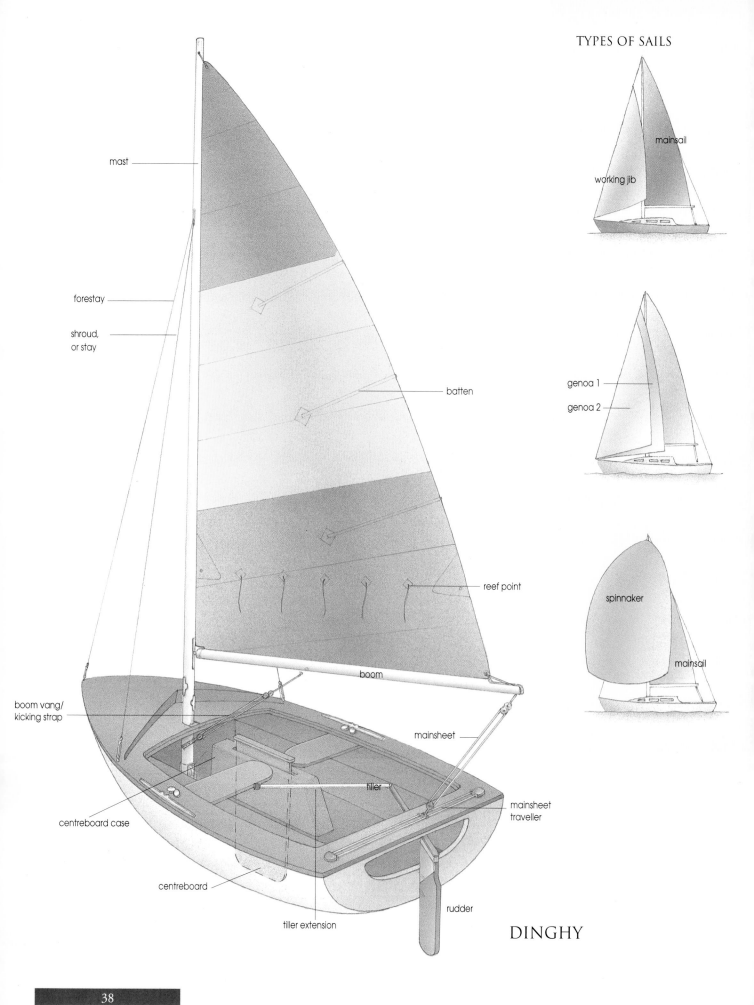

TYPES OF SAILS

mainsail

working jib

genoa 1

genoa 2

spinnaker

mainsail

mast

forestay

shroud,
or stay

batten

reef point

boom

boom vang/
kicking strap

mainsheet

tiller

mainsheet
traveller

centreboard case

centreboard

rudder

tiller extension

DINGHY

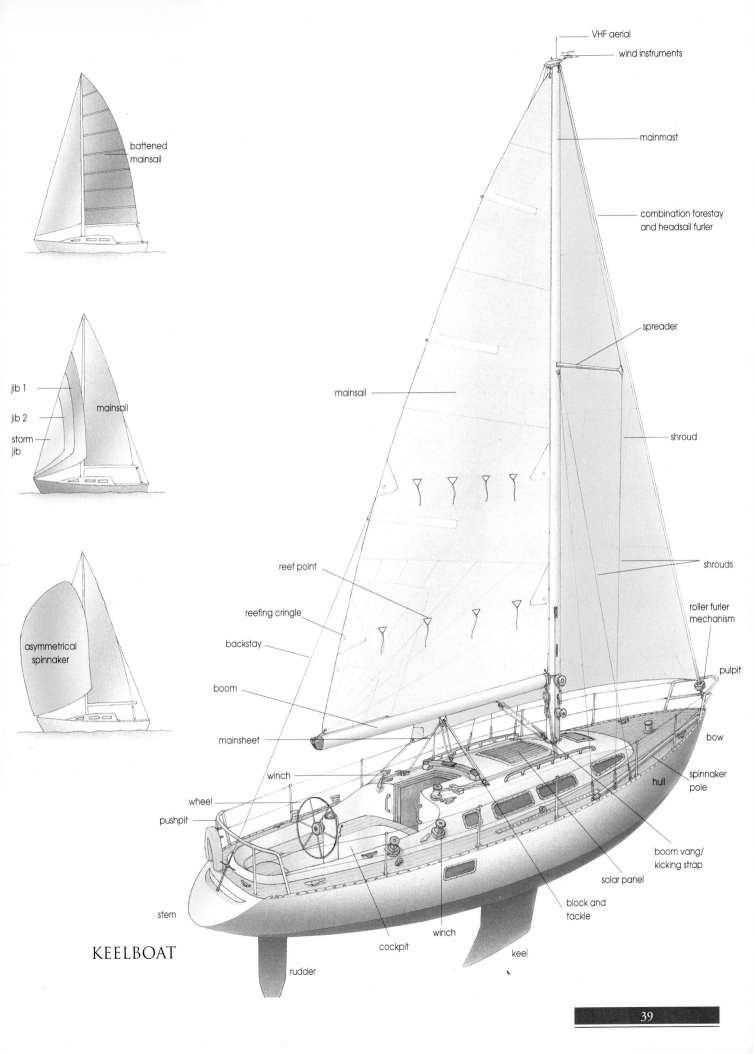

battened
mainsail

jib 1

jib 2

storm
jib

mainsail

asymmetrical
spinnaker

VHF aerial

wind instruments

mainmast

combination forestay
and headsail furler

spreader

mainsail

shroud

shrouds

reef point

reefing cringle

roller furler
mechanism

backstay

pulpit

boom

mainsheet

bow

winch

spinnaker
pole

wheel

hull

pushpit

boom vang/
kicking strap

solar panel

block and
tackle

stern

winch

cockpit

keel

rudder

KEELBOAT

A centreboard's primary role is to prevent a vessel from being blown sideways. Dinghies have either a pivoted centreboard, housed in a centreboard case, or the more simple daggerboard which is not pivoted but slides down the centreboard case. Going downwind, the dagger- or centreboard can be almost fully raised.

Steering
The vessel is steered by a rudder which pivots, and is controlled by a tiller (in smaller vessels). This angles the rudder left or right of the centreline to turn the craft (when angled to the left, the craft will veer to the left). Larger craft are equipped with a wheel rather than a tiller. Rudders, centreboards and keels are often referred to as 'foils'.

SAIL TRIM AND SHAPE
The shape of a sail is very important if you want to get optimum performance from it. A typical cross-section of a mainsail is shown in the illustration on page 57. Note the chord depth, or draft, midway from the leading edge – the wind is filling the sail in the first illustration. Many sailors have their own ideas of exactly what the chord depth should be, and whether the maximum depth should be near the leading edge, near the middle, or points in between. Few believe the draft should be aft of the centre.

One aspect is not in dispute – the fact that full sails (maximum draft) are required for light winds, and that they should be progressively flatter as the wind speed increases. This is borne out once more by aircraft wings: most commercial passenger jet airliners have both leading and trailing edge flaps. When fully extended, they increase the wing chord and draught, dramatically increasing lift for slow-speed flying, such as is required for landing. Conversely, at high speeds, the flaps are fully retracted.

Telltales
Fine strands of spinnaker cloth or wool on the sail, known as telltales, give an excellent indication of whether or not a sail is working efficiently to windward. Telltales are normally set slightly behind the luff of the sail. They should be different colours on different sides of the sail, preferably red for port and green for starboard. If the sail is set correctly, and the boat is pointing at the most efficient angle to the wind, the telltales will be horizontal. If the telltale on

Red = windward
Green = leeward

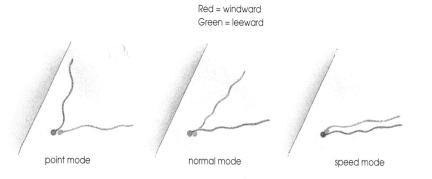

point mode   normal mode   speed mode

TELLTALES

the windward side of the sail lifts or starts to flutter, you are pointing too close to the wind. Conversely, if the leeward telltale lifts, you can head up and point closer to the wind. Telltales are an invaluable aid to the racing sailor, but they have their place on non-racing boats as well – the helmsman will get more satisfaction from his sport if he is able to sail his boat more efficiently.

Weather Helm

One of the terms a sailor will learn early on is 'weather helm'. This is the tendency of a boat to round up to windward, and must be countered by pulling the tiller up to windward to correct the boat's course. A little weather helm is good, because it helps give the helmsman that elusive 'feel', so necessary to him becoming good in his role. There are many factors contributing to weather helm – two being the position of the mast and the position of the centreboard or keel. The major contributor to weather helm is the shape of the boat when heeled. A symmetrical hull will go straight when upright, but as soon as the boat is heeled, the hull lines presented to the water are asymmetrical and the hull has a tendency to turn.

Therefore, one of the key factors in minimizing weather helm when it blows hard is to sail the boat as flat (upright) as possible. As the wind increases, continue to depower the rig – that is, flatten the sails with the several methods at your disposal.

Helm Control in Wind Shifts The wind very rarely remains in exactly the same direction for very long. Therefore, a sailboat moving along an exactly straight course on the beat is probably not being sailed efficiently. The helmsman, when sailing to windward, must head the boat up in the lifts, and pull off when the wind heads. The course of the boat will be constantly varied slightly to sail at maximum efficiency. For the cruising man who is not the least bit interested in optimum performance, however, this is not essential.

Remember that every time the helm is moved, the rudder, presented at an angle to the water flow, tends to slow the boat. A fairly gentle touch is needed, with firmness rather than abruptness or roughness necessary for manoeuvring. There are occasions when more positive, even violent, helm movements are required, these being avoiding a collision or a broach (*see* page 49), or promoting

planing. When reaching, or sailing off the wind, the same fluctuations in wind direction will occur. Here the sails may be left in a constant trim position, and the boat luffed or pulled off in the wind shifts, or the boat can be sailed on a straight course and the sails eased or sheeted in, as may be appropriate. Alternatively a combination of trimming the sails and altering course may be used.

Trimming the sails has become second nature to the racing sailor. Beginners will not get into trouble, however, by failing to react to every small wind shift. Simply be aware of them and for those who want to become competitive sailors, take account of them.

Above *A correctly trimmed boat, with the rudder centred.*

Opposite top *Note the telltales and camber stripes.*

THE POINTS OF SAILING

The figure of 45 degrees to the true wind is an approximation. Different types of craft and different types of rigs have varying pointing abilities. The most modern hi-tech racing yacht will point much closer to the wind than a sturdy cruising yacht.

Beating Sailing as close as possible to the wind, called beating to windward, involves sheeting the sails close to the centreline.

Reaching Heading the boat off, or away from, the wind until the wind is at right angles to the boat is known as reaching, or sailing across the wind. On modern cruise yachts and dinghies, reaching is the fastest point of sailing. To trim sails to the optimum on a reach, trim them again so that the telltales are parallel, or the luff of the sail is just starting to lift (if telltales are not fitted, the luff of the sail will give you the same indications, but is not as sensitive). If the luff lifts or shakes, sheet in (pull in the rope, or sheet, that controls the sail) slightly. Test the set of your sails by heading the boat up a little to see if the telltales lift, or the luff shakes, and then head off a

POINTS OF SAILING

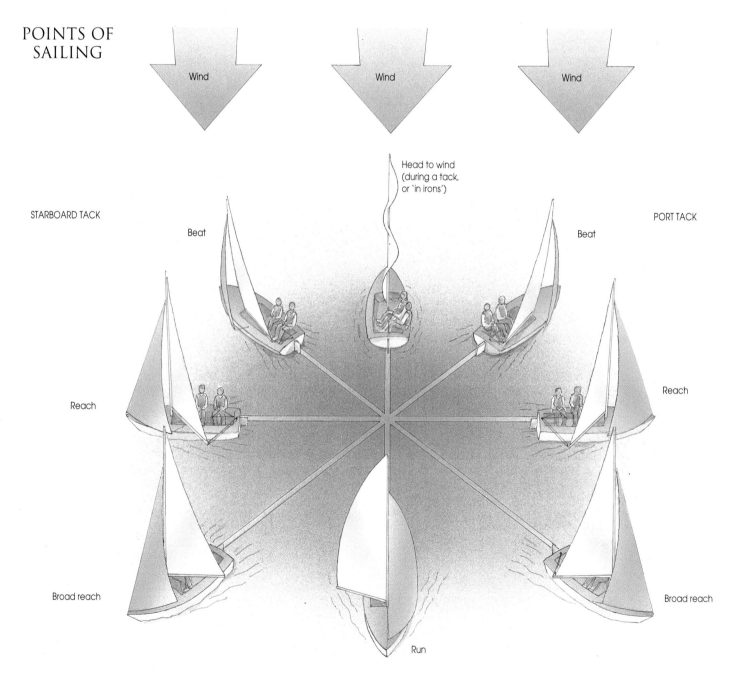

Wind

Wind

Wind

Head to wind
(during a tack,
or 'in irons')

STARBOARD TACK

PORT TACK

Beat

Beat

Reach

Reach

Broad reach

Broad reach

Run

position. On a run, it is obviously not needed to stop sideways motion, but it should be lowered a few inches to help prevent rolling and this will assist the boat to track (keep its course) more easily.

Wind direction indicators (or Windexes) are usually placed at the top of the mast.

little again. Or, instead of changing course, ease or haul in the sails to test wind angles. Another invaluable tool to help you assess wind direction is a burgee or Windex at the masthead. Burgees (triangular flags) were once quite common, but most sailboats these days carry purpose-made, sensitive, wind direction indicators, commonly known as Windexes. Most offshore racers carry electronic equipment giving wind speed and wind direction.

Broad Reaching By bearing away (heading downwind) some more, sailors will attain the broad reach position. The sails are further eased, and when the wind is strong enough, this is the sailing angle at which most dinghies will plane.

Running Pulling off still further you will attain the running position, with the wind exactly astern. Here the sails are eased to their furthest extent. Some people put a knot in the end of their mainsheet so the sail cannot be eased too far. 'Running dead' before the wind is something you will not do very often. If there are any waves, it is all too easy to head off too far, which could result in an involuntary gybe as the wind catches the sail from the other side. This can result in a bang on the head for the crew or, in a dinghy, a capsize.

Many small craft are sloop-rigged, that is, they have a mainsail and jib. When running, the jib is under the lee of the mainsail. It is deprived of wind and does little work in this position. It can be held out on the windward side, or better still, poled out. This is known as goosewinging and will add to the speed and stability of a dinghy running downwind.

Centreboard Positions When sailing to windward, the centreboard should be in the full down position. The sideways force generated is at its maximum on this point of sailing and the centreboard counteracts this. On a reach, it can be raised to about the half-up

Left *An International 14 is reaching with an asymmetric spinnaker set.*

Below *This boat is beating to windward with its sails sheeted in hard.*

Above, right and below
These sailors are getting the best out of their boats through effective use of crew weight.

IMPORTANCE OF CREW WEIGHT

Crew weight plays a major role in dinghies. When going to windward, the heeling force (the angle a boat adopts to the vertical) of the wind is greatest. In anything other than a light breeze, the crew will need to be on the weather (windward) side – probably all that's required in a cruising dinghy. In racing dinghies it will be necessary to sit, or hike out, with feet under the toestraps. Trapeze dinghies carry a wire that supports the weight of a crewman leaning out on the windward side (*see* page 103); the trapeze is used to aid the boat to sail to windward in all conditions, from moderate weather upwards. As the wind increases, the crew weight, of course, does not.

The many ways of reducing the heeling force of the rig are covered later in Chapter Four.

Most dinghies, and indeed, ocean racers for that matter, sail fastest when they are upright, or close to upright. To get the best out of a sailboat going to windward, it is best to sail it as level as possible (except on a very calm day when it may pay to heel the boat a little to get gravity to assist in shaping the sails). Again, the crew weight can assist. (Even in keelboats and ocean racers the crew sits up on the weather rail on the beat.) As the dinghy is pulled off the wind, the crew sits upright, or moves inboard until balance is achieved. On a run, a crew member may sit on each side of the boat, or all members may sit in the middle.

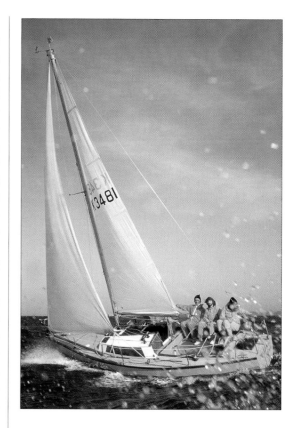

Keeping the boat trimmed in the horizontal plane (on a longitudinal axis) is also important. Should one sit too far aft (near the stern of the boat), the bow would probably be too high, while the bottom of the transom might be submerged, increasing drag. If one sits too far forward, the transom may be clear of the water, the bow too deep and the boat could well be unstable. Correctly trimmed, the boat will be at its most stable and will sail at its best.

In addition, keep the crew close together to avoid the 'seesaw' effect. If one imagines two children in the normal position on a seesaw, when each child kicks up with his or her feet, a seesaw motion is induced. Should the children be moved inwards until they are both sitting close to the pivot point, that seesaw movement will be much reduced, if not impossible to achieve.

Pitching has the result of slowing a boat down but correct crew weight minimizes this. On a dinghy, pitching can be counteracted with the crew sitting or trapezing close together. On a keelboat or offshore racer, keep as much weight as possible towards the centre of the boat. A more comfortable motion will result, and the boat will go faster.

BASIC MANOEUVRES

The basic manoeuvres discussed here (*see* illustrations) are covered from the point of view of a stable type of dinghy. Once most sailors have mastered dinghy sailing, it doesn't take long to apply the knowledge to other types of craft.

Slowing Down

Bear in mind that a sailboat has no brakes or the handy reverse gear available to the powerboat operator. This can be quite frightening during the learning period while one is sailing in a crowded anchorage, approaching the shore or a narrow launching and retrieving slipway. Several methods of slowing down are available to the sailor. The first, unless the boat is running, is to ease the sheets. With sails flapping, the boat will be able to come to a near stop. If you are close reaching, or beating to windward, luff the boat up (that is, head up the boat towards the wind) in addition to easing the sheets. The luffing technique can also be used to approach a jetty from downwind, or to pick up a mooring.

Heaving to will keep you nearly stationary with a slight drift to leeward. To do this, back the jib, or headsail – that is, sheet the jib to the windward side. When you ease the mainsail, the boat will ride in a most docile manner.

Tacking

The next manoeuvre – a simple one – is tacking, or going about (*see* also page 104). The helmsman of a dinghy will have the tiller, or the tiller extension, in one hand and the mainsheet in the other. The helmsman alerts the crew by calling 'Stand by' or 'Stand by to tack'. The helmsman's next call is 'lee oh', after which he pushes the helm steadily down (away from him). The boat heads up, passes through the head-to-wind position. The tiller is brought back to the centreline, and the boat heads off on the opposite tack.

During the tack, the crew and helmsman must cross to the other side of the boat. The helmsman can face forward or aft during the tack; this will often be influenced by whether the mainsail is aft- or centre-sheeted (*see* illustration right). During this period, the helmsman will change hands, the tiller going from one hand to the other, and the mainsheet going to the opposite hand. It may sound really complicated, but it is not; it simply takes a little practice.

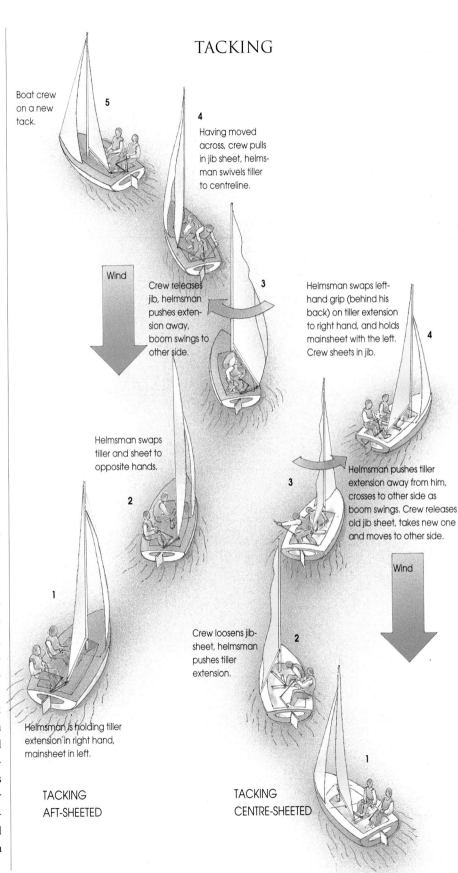

TACKING

Boat crew on a new tack.

5

4 Having moved across, crew pulls in jib sheet, helmsman swivels tiller to centreline.

Wind

Crew releases jib, helmsman pushes extension away, boom swings to other side.

3

Helmsman swaps left-hand grip (behind his back) on tiller extension to right hand, and holds mainsheet with the left. Crew sheets in jib.

4

Helmsman swaps tiller and sheet to opposite hands.

2

3

Helmsman pushes tiller extension away from him, crosses to other side as boom swings. Crew releases old jib sheet, takes new one and moves to other side.

Wind

1

Crew loosens jib-sheet, helmsman pushes tiller extension.

2

Helmsman is holding tiller extension in right hand, mainsheet in left.

1

TACKING
AFT-SHEETED

TACKING
CENTRE-SHEETED

GYBING

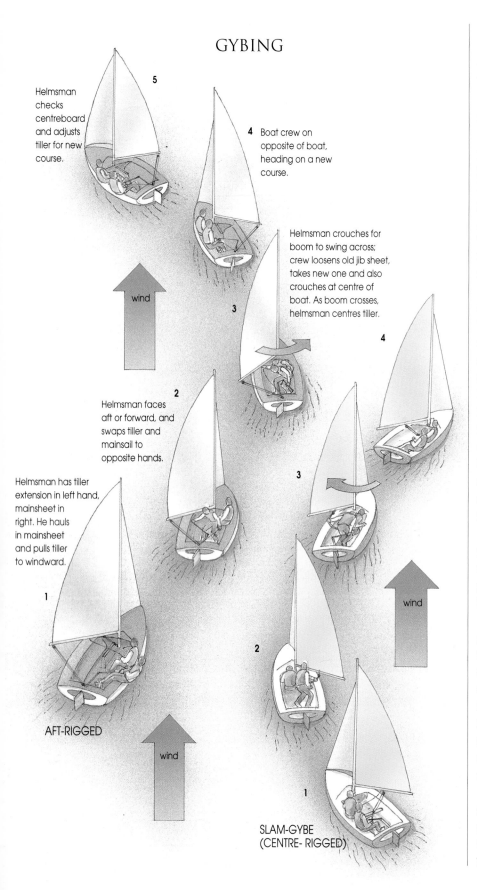

5 Helmsman checks centreboard and adjusts tiller for new course.

4 Boat crew on opposite of boat, heading on a new course.

Helmsman crouches for boom to swing across; crew loosens old jib sheet, takes new one and also crouches at centre of boat. As boom crosses, helmsman centres tiller.

3

wind

2 Helmsman faces aft or forward, and swaps tiller and mainsail to opposite hands.

4

Helmsman has tiller extension in left hand, mainsheet in right. He hauls in mainsheet and pulls tiller to windward.

3

1

wind

2

AFT-RIGGED

wind

1

SLAM-GYBE (CENTRE-RIGGED)

If the tiller is not held over long enough, or if it is a choppy day, the boat may 'miss stays' – that is, it may not go about. If this happens, sheet in, get the boat going and try again.

Alternatively, you could end up 'in irons' (making no progress, or lying 'dead in the water'). A light dinghy will rapidly start going backwards. To complete the tack, reverse the rudder or back the jib to push the bow around. In a cat-rigged boat (that is, it has only a mainsail), the alternative of backing the jib is not available, so only the rudder can be used to get out of 'irons'. Years ago, when sailing dinghies were sluggish and heavy, getting into irons was common. With today's efficient sailing dinghies, it does not often happen.

Gybing

This is a much more difficult manoeuvre than tacking. Here, the boat is running (heading downwind) and the course is altered to bring the wind across the stern (from one side of the boat to the other). Instead of a few flaps of the sail which you get in the head-to-wind position while tacking, the wind takes the sail and slams it to the opposite side. If not executed correctly, a gybe can result in a knock on the head from the boom for the helmsman or crew member, and in heavy winds, a capsize. You can almost always tack instead of gybing if you have sufficient room. This is an option if it is blowing hard.

Practise gybing in light weather first – and perfect your technique before trying a gybe in strong winds (*see* also page 104). When practising, do not try to gybe from a dead run to a dead run. Rather go from a broad reach (or a training run) back to a broad reach.

To gybe, commence with the words, 'Stand by to gybe'. On the words 'gybe oh', assuming you are on the windward side, pull the tiller towards yourself (this is the opposite manoeuvre to tacking). At the same time sheet in the mainsail. As the wind takes it from the opposite side, move to that side of the boat, keeping your head low. If the boat wants to round up (or head up into the wind), correct firmly with the helm, ease the mainsheet and settle onto the new course.

Don't gybe with the centreboard fully down; it should be about three-quarters raised. Equally, do not gybe with the centreboard fully raised either – the boat will roll very easily, which could contribute to a capsize.

APPARENT WIND

So far when we have talked about wind direction, it is the true wind to which we have been referring – that is, the direction from which the wind is blowing if the observer is standing still. Once a sailboat gathers way, its progress 'modifies' the direction of the wind. This is best understood by the illustration below, showing smoke from a tugboat. The modified wind direction is known as the 'apparent wind'. It is the apparent wind to which the sails of a boat have to be trimmed.

In the slower types of dinghies and keelboats, not too much attention need be paid to the apparent wind, but in fast boats such as multihulls, the new-generation skiff-type dinghies, sports boats and off-shore maxis, the apparent wind plays a major role in sail setting and tactics. As a boat moves forward, the apparent wind moves ahead, or heads the boat more. An efficient dinghy sailing at 40 degrees off the true wind may in fact be sailing at 30 degrees off the apparent wind.

An extremely fast boat will move the apparent wind well forward. A skiff-type dinghy, planing at high speed on a reach, could be sheeted in nearly as hard as she would be on the beat. The effect of apparent wind impacts on downwind technique greatly. If one sails too deep (too far off the wind), the high speeds achieved by the type of boat described above drop off rapidly. The fastest course for these boats is to tack downwind on a series of reaches, gybing at the end of each reach.

Not only is the direction of the apparent wind different to that of the true wind, but so is its strength. A sailboat, beating to windward at 5 knots of boat speed in a 15-knot true wind, is experiencing an apparent wind of around 20 knots. Conversely, a sailboat running free with a boat speed of 5 knots in a 15-knot true wind will experience an apparent wind of about 10 knots, half of what occurs on the beat. Sometimes running can lull you into a false sense of security and it is a rude awakening when you head upwind and experience the greatly increased apparent wind strength.

Even if you are not sailing the hi-tech boats on which apparent wind plays such a major factor, do bear it in mind nonetheless. After all, your telltales and Windex will operate according to the apparent wind. Ocean racers and boats such as those which compete in events like the America's Cup have sophisticated and accurate instruments which give the wind direction and strength for both true and apparent winds.

Mast Bend

How is it possible to change the shape of a Dacron sail that has had its form built into it by having the panels of cloth from which it was made specially moulded? Mast bend is the primary way of flattening, or reducing the chord of, a mainsail (*see* page 57). These days most dinghies have rigs which are set up to allow the mast to bend as wind strength increases, automatically flattening the sail.

The small keelboat classes and offshore racers can usually induce mast bend when the backstay is tensioned. Many sailors also set their rigs up with some pre-bend, and this aspect is used to ensure the rig bends correctly when the backstay is tensioned by a crew member. Pre-bend is particularly easy to achieve when masts are keel stepped (fittings on the boat into which the heel of the mast fits).

A modern rig set up with some pre-bend.

APPARENT WIND

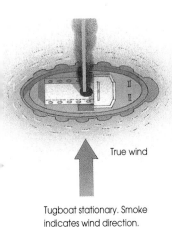

True wind

Tugboat stationary. Smoke indicates wind direction.

True wind   Apparent wind

Tugboat at moderate speed.

True wind

Tugboat at maximum speed. Apparent wind at maximum deflection from true wind.

Apparent wind

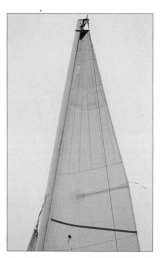

Camber stripe and black band at head of spar.

A Cunningham cringle.

The boom vang, or kicking strap.

Black Bands

Most classes of yacht have black bands painted on their spars. This is to ensure that no-one has sails that are larger in area than is allowed by the class rules. Hoisting the sail right up to the top black band and to the black band at the end of the boom, will ensure that the mainsail is as flat as possible, before other methods are used. In light weather the sail need not necessarily be fully hoisted, or pulled out to the end of the boom, which allows for a fuller shape.

The Cunningham Cringle

As wind strength increases, the draft in the mainsail tends to move aft; it should however be kept reasonably far forward. A Cunningham cringle (also known as a Cunningham eye) and downhaul tackle at the base of the mainsail will help do this job. The Cunningham is tensioned, which tightens the luff and moves the draft of the sail forward. This device was named after its American inventor, Briggs Cunningham, who first used it many years ago. It is found on dinghies, maxi yachts and even on some radio-controlled models.

The Boom Vang

The boom vang (also known as a 'kicking strap') in its simplest form is a block and tackle attached to the foot of the mast at deck level, and to a point on the boom. The boom vang has a number of functions. By holding the boom down, it keeps the mainsail from twisting, keeps the leech (aft side or trailing edge of sail) tight, and generally enables you to get more power out of the mainsail. A very important downwind function is to keep the boom under control, not only in reaching, broad reaching and running, but during a gybe. Prior to boom vangs, gybing was much more difficult, and Chinese gybes, resulting in a portion of the mainsail being at each side of the mast, sometimes occurred. For serious racing, the boom vang is a major tool in optimizing boat speed.

Mainsheet Traveller

Many dinghies, and most offshore boats – at least those intended to do some racing – will have a mainsheet traveller. In light weather, the mainsheet will probably be sheeted with the lower blocks (or pulleys) on the centreline; high-pointing keelboats may even sheet with the blocks slightly to windward. As the wind strengthens, the boat can be depowered and optimum speed can be maintained by dropping the mainsheet blocks to leeward.

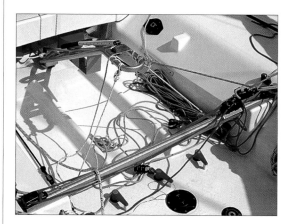

Above *A mainsheet traveller on a First Class Solo.*

Camber Stripes

Many of the procedures for depowering the sails/rig involve flattening the mainsail. Earlier, the chord of the sail was discussed. Camber stripes – sewn, glued or drawn with a felt-tipped pen onto the sail in contrasting colours – give a good picture of sail shape (camber being the slightly convex curve of the sail's surface). Experts watch the shape of their sails constantly, and adjust them as wind speeds and sea conditions change.

Camber stripes are used mainly on mainsails and headsails: a typical dinghy mainsail may have two camber stripes, a larger keelboat mainsail three. With fully battened mainsails, the batten can take the place of camber stripes. Photographs, taken in different conditions looking up from a point under the boom, are a good indication of how the sail changes. Black pen can be used to draw in the chord on the photographs, and depth and position can be compared for different wind strengths. If sails need to be altered, such photographs can be a guide for the sail maker.

Camber stripes on a sail.

DIFFICULT SITUATIONS
Broaching

Broaching occurs when control of a sailboat is lost while sailing off the wind (and sometimes also on the wind). It almost always happens in strong winds. The boat heels over, resulting in a great deal of weather helm, and rounds rapidly up into the wind. In a dinghy, a broach could well result in a capsize. Some of the factors which can cause or contribute to a broach are:

- the mainsheet getting caught and the sail being sheeted in too tightly on changing course (gybing)
- the tiller not being centred soon enough, causing the boat to round up (turn towards the wind) more than anticipated
- the crew not having moved correctly to balance the boat
- the centreboard having been lowered too far
- heavy rolling while travelling downwind
- having too great a sail area for the conditions.

The following quick action could prevent a capsize in the above scenarios:

- freeing the mainsheet and easing it rapidly (often referred to as 'dumping the mainsheet')
- ensuring effective use of crew weight; moving crew weight to the windward side with the tiller pulled hard over to windward
- checking centreboard position.

If you are overpowered on a reach and a broach commences, get all your weight to windward and ease the sheets fully. You may then regain control and be able to resume your previous course.

Left *This boat has just broached.*

Capsizing

Capsizing is something which will almost certainly happen to those who sail dinghies (or catamarans, as the photographs of a Hobie Cat below indicate). Part of your learning procedure should be to capsize your dinghy in calm weather, and learn the ins and outs of righting it. A word of warning on this point: wear a buoyancy aid. These days they are not bulky and can save lives – even good swimmers can be temporarily stunned by a blow to the head.

Almost all dinghies can be righted by their crews without outside assistance (although this has not always been the case). Some are constructed so that they will float on their sides without taking any water, others will partially flood, but the flotation, either built in or in the form of buoyancy bags, will keep the boat afloat. Once she is righted, she can be bailed out, or the suction bailers can remove the water if the boat is sailed fast enough.

The most important thing is to prevent the boat from going upside down. In a single-handed boat, a 'dry' capsize is sometimes possible. As the boat goes over, the helmsman steps onto the centreboard, and is in a position to right the boat immediately. If the helmsman, together with a crewman in a two-man boat, tries to climb onto the centreboard a little too late, their weight may be so positioned that they aid the boat to turn upside down.

There is no one way to carry out a righting sequence. However, a good technique for a two-man

craft, and one taught by many sailing schools, is the 'scoop method'. Both the helmsman and crew member are in the water, between the boat and the boom. Swim to the transom. The crew member may need to hold the rudder with a twisting movement to help prevent the boat inverting. Taking the mainsheet as a lifeline, the helmsman swims round to the centreboard, holds onto it or climbs onto it. The crewman then throws the helmsman the weather jib sheet, which the helmsman uses to obtain more leverage to pull the boat upright. The crewman lies on the leeward side of the boat and is 'scooped' in as the boat rights.

There are many variants of this technique, particularly among the racing sailors, who want to get back into the race with the minimum waste of time. If the person going to stand on the centreboard is comfortable in the water, or is a good swimmer, he or she can push him- or herself under the boat in the vicinity of the centreboard, saving the time of swimming around the boat. In a boat which floats 'dry', the crewman in the water to leeward can climb up to the weather side at the appropriate moment. When the boat is upright, take stock of your surroundings so as to avoid drifting onto other craft, sandbanks and buoys.

If you are unfortunate enough to turn fully upside down, you can get the boat back to 90 degrees by getting the crew to stand together on the same gunwale, holding onto a jib sheet.

Opposite *Sails are eased to slow the boat down as a man is retrieved from the water.*

Below and below right
Sailors prepare to right a Hobie 16 that has capsized (more difficult than a monohull). If the boat can be positioned head-to-wind, the wind passing under the sail can assist in righting it.

MAN OVERBOARD

A man going overboard from a dinghy is not uncommon. The helmsman or crewman could miss the toestraps and somersault backwards, or a trapeze wire or harness could break. If this occurs in strong winds in a two-man dinghy, there is a good chance that the boat will capsize. If it does, the person in the water will probably be close enough to the boat to swim back to it.

If the weather is moderate enough for the boat to be sailed by the person remaining on board, he or she will have to manage the boat as well as pick up the person in the water. Gybing a two-man boat single-handedly, except in very light weather, is probably asking for trouble; it is better to tack. Sail away from the person in the water with sheets partially eased to avoid being overpowered. Tack, sail to leeward of the person and luff up, passing the person to leeward, enabling him or her to board on the windward side. Remember to keep your speed down, and the boat under control when approaching the person in the water.

It is well worth practising a 'man overboard' drill, using something that floats, until you are fully confident that you have the procedure well in hand. The same applies to keelboat and offshore sailing (*see* Seamanship and Safety, Chapter Nine). Losing a man overboard out at sea could be very serious if the crew is not familiar with some of the many ways to recover a person.

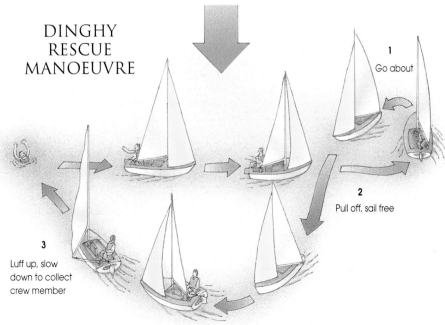

DINGHY RESCUE MANOEUVRE

1 Go about

2 Pull off, sail free

3 Luff up, slow down to collect crew member

CHAPTER FOUR

THE EVOLUTION OF MODERN SAILBOATS

HULL DEVELOPMENT

Sailboats have developed continuously over the years. Modern sailboat designs have become increasingly faster. The main reason for this is that better power-to-weight ratios have been made possible by using lighter hi-tech materials in the building of boats, and through better use of ballast, whether it be in the form of a bulb at the bottom of an ocean racer's keel, or human ballast in the form of an entire dinghy crew out on trapeze. Also playing a major role is the improvement in sail cloths, sail design and their controllability.

The innovative use of movable water ballast in such craft as the Whitbread 60s – where water is pumped into special tanks on the windward side, increasing stability which equates to adding power and sail-carrying ability – has added a great deal of speed to these boats. In one respect, sailboats are no different from aeroplanes or Formula 1 racing cars: build them lighter and add more power – in this case, sail area – and they will go faster.

As the weight of sailboats has decreased over the past 30 years, so the shape of the hull has also had to change. The older, heavier boats had to have fairly

Above *A John Corby-designed offshore racing yacht going to windward.*

deep, full-bodied hulls to support the weight of boat, gear and crew. Many of these boats, particularly keelboats, sailed permanently in displacement mode (they did not rise up in the water and plane). Displacement boats, as has been mentioned earlier, have their maximum speed governed by the formula: 1.4 multiplied by the square root of LWL in feet (LWL being the length of the waterline).

A modern Open 60 beats to windward. These large, very fast boats are used in round-the-world single-handed races.

Looking at offshore racing yacht designs of 50 years ago, we find that a yacht with an overall length of 35ft (10.6m) might have had a waterline length of 24ft (7.3m). She would have had long bow and stern overhangs, producing a profile which many consider to be beautiful; the appearance of those boats is referred to as 'classic'. Today's offshore racer of 35ft (10.6m) is more likely to have a waterline length of some 30ft (9.1m). Not taking other factors into account, this increased waterline length means her top displacement speed is far greater than that of her 50-year-old sister. She is also probably beamier (wider) and has more inherent stability. This improves her sail-carrying power, which means she has been designed with a far larger sail area than her earlier sister. As the modern boat has been built

Above *Modern sailboats in the Sportsboat Class begin a race in the French SPI Quest regatta.*

much lighter, she also has a much flatter hull shape. This does not have nearly the same water resistance as the older boat, and does not drag a large wake at high hull speeds.

Today's boat is almost certainly a fin keeler with a separate rudder, while her predecessor had 'wine-glass-shaped' hull sections, with a keel incorporated into the hull as an integral part of the hull structure, together with a rudder hinged at the back of the keel.

As the offshore keelboats have developed, so has their ability to surf. High surfing speeds on waves in heavy weather have been recorded during recent times. The power-to-weight ratio of some of the modern ocean racers, for instance Whitbread 60s, is such that they are capable of genuine planing, just like a dinghy.

Although offshore (or ocean) racers have been described here, the trend has also filtered through to cruising boats. Most cruising sailboats today have fin keels and separate rudders. They are on the whole much faster than their predecessors and, as many people believe, easier to sail.

As waterline lengths and beams have increased, and modern construction has eliminated complex and bulky internal framing, the internal volumes of a given size of sailboat have increased dramatically. The accommodation offered in today's stock cruisers is positively luxurious compared to that of 50 years ago.

But this does not mean there is no place for a 'classic', or traditional, boat today. While they will not be that fast on the race course, they can cross oceans safely and have a loyal following among the cruising yacht fraternity. They also offer pride of ownership, much like a veteran car. Several yacht-building companies specialize in heavy-displacement, traditional cruising yachts, and find a ready market for their craft.

Computers in Sailboat Design Progress made in the development of sailboats has been assisted and accelerated by the use of computers, which can draw and 'fair' a lines plan (represent a three-dimensional yacht in two dimensions using a series of lines), perform complex calculations and produce printed plans in a fraction of the time previously taken by naval architects or yacht designers.

In addition, Velocity Prediction Programs (VPPs) have been developed which enable the designers (again using computer programs) to calculate the speeds of the craft they are designing, on various points of sailing. They can then vary their designs – a decidedly faster process today with computers – and run the modified design through the VPP. In this way sailboat designs can be largely optimized before they are launched.

In terms of sail design, too, computer programs have been produced which are able to provide accurate dimensions for the forming of panels in a desired shape. The shape required, the depth of chord at various heights, the position of maximum draft and other factors are programmed in, and the computer produces the information necessary to cut the panels.

It wasn't long ago that changes in sailboat characteristics took years to emerge. The designers took their best designs of a season, modified them slightly and then had to wait until the new boats went out and sailed to see what improvements, if any, had been achieved. Computers have probably made sailboat design more costly, but the speed of development has been given a tremendous boost.

Dinghies

The dinghy has gone through a very similar evolution to offshore sailboats, the breakthrough similarly being weight reduction and sail-carrying ability. The increase of hi-tech construction in top-level sailing dinghies has allowed the development of flatter, faster hulls. In the early days of planing dinghies, the

FRANK BETHWAITE

As Uffa Fox was considered to be the father of the planing dinghy, so Australian Frank Bethwaite should be considered the father of today's high-performance skiff-type dinghies. He has been at the leading edge of national and world-class sailing for over 50 years. His interests and career were ideally suited to the development of fast sailboats, as they included aeronautical engineering and meteorology. He spent 30 years of his life in military and civil aviation, and scientific flying, while his hobbies included sailing, developing high-speed sailboats, and flying model gliders as well as full-size sailplanes. When Bethwaite retired from flying, he put a great deal of energy into his objective to produce a viable sailboat that would circumnavigate a round-the-buoys course faster than the speed of wind.

18ft (5.5m) skiffs in Sydney Harbour, Australia.

This has now been achieved in the skiff-type dinghy – the breakthrough was the discovery that boats could plane to windward. He conducted many experiments, most of them in Sydney Harbour, which are described in his book, *High Performance Sailing* (Waterline).

Frank Bethwaite produced a family of champion sailors – his children between them have won three Olympic sailing medals and have also been world champions in no fewer than four different classes. Over the years, Bethwaite has done much design work on the Sydney Harbour 18s – the original high-speed skiffs – regularly sailed by his son Julian. It is therefore no real surprise to learn that Julian has designed the International 49er, a class of two-man skiff which will compete as an Olympic Class for the first time in Sydney in 2000.

---

crew often had to move aft to promote planing. These boats tended to plane in a 'bow up' attitude, limiting top speeds. As the modern boats have become flatter, or have less 'rocker', they plane in a much more level attitude and reach higher speeds.

Development in the ultralight modern skiff-type dinghy which is becoming so popular today owes much to the staggering evolution of the Sydney Harbour 18ft (5.5m) skiff. These boats, with few limitations on design, are incredibly fast. Once they had many crew members to handle their vast sail plans; today they have crews of two or three, trapezing from wing-like structures, handling the dinghies' huge sails with comparative ease.

Modern Sports Boats
Sports boats appeared in the early 1990s. They are relatively small, most are about 24–25ft (7.3–7.6m) long, they are lightly built of hi-tech materials, and they have ballast keels, sometimes retractable.

In addition, they have large sail areas. These new-generation small keelboats have high power-to-weight ratios and are astoundingly fast. The first of these boats was the Melges 24, named after Buddy

Below *Melges 24s being sailed in the UK.*

BRUCE FARR

Bruce Farr is a New Zealander by birth, and in his younger days was a well-known sailor in Auckland. Today he is one of the world's top yacht designers. His designs first came to the attention of sailors in the early 1970s when his boats started winning races in New Zealand. It wasn't long before Bruce Farr designs were representing his native country in the prestigious Admiral's Cup series, held every second year in the UK.

By the end of the 1970s, Farr was an established designer, producing highly successful raceboats to the IOR (International Offshore Rule), which was the major rating system of that time. In the early 1980s he moved his design office from Auckland to Annapolis, USA.

With the demise of the IOR, the IMS (International Measurement System) was established, and Bruce Farr and Associates soon became a force to be reckoned with, designing many race-winning IMS boats. Farr himself is involved in the hull lines of all the boats his office creates. His design practice is absolutely up to date in terms of the latest computer technology, but yacht design still requires the 'human touch' – technology on its own won't produce a race-winning yacht.

Farr has in recent years contributed a number of notable one-designs to the international sailing scene. Among these are the Mumm 30, the Mumm 36, the Farr 40 and the Correl 45 – fast, competitive boats which, in each class, produce pure one-design racing. With the possible exception of the Mumm 36, the sail plan and deck layouts are kept as simple as possible.

Bruce Farr and Associates have also been involved in the design of some highly successful America's Cup yachts. However, the area in which they have absolutely swept the board is in the Whitbread Round-the-World Race. For the 1997/98 race, the Farr office produced the designs for eight of the nine boats that were successful in completing the course.

Beneteau of France, prolific builder of popular yachts – many of which are used by the world's big charter yacht companies – has a number of Farr designs in its range. In the contemporary market, Farr designs probably make a similar impact to the decades when the US Sparkman and Stephens designs were a dominant force in the sailing world.

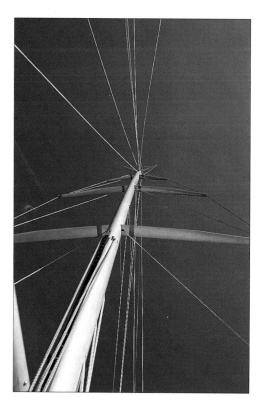

Melges, a well-known American sailor. He was the principal helmsman of *America³*, which won the America's Cup in 1993. The design team that created *America³* included the US design company, Reichel and Pugh. Together, Buddy Melges, John Reichel and Jim Pugh dreamed up the astonishing Melges 24. It was an immediate success and has rapidly developed into a major international class. The speed increase over existing small keelboats of a similar size is nothing short of amazing.

The term 'sports boat' suitably describes the new breed of small keelboat. This new aspect of the sport has succeeded in enlisting many new supporters around the world to sports-boat sailing.

FOILS (KEELS, CENTREBOARDS AND RUDDERS)

Foils, as keels and rudders are also known, have played a major role in the speed increases in racing craft, and the development has filtered through to cruising yachts. As keels have become more efficient, they have developed more lift for a given area (the wetted surface of keels has been reduced), thus adding to the speed of the craft.

Rudders, too, have improved, and are less likely to stall out (a stalled rudder creates turbulence in the water, reducing its ability to steer). They can give good control at speeds from 1 to 25 knots or more.

RIG DEVELOPMENT
Wood and Aluminium Masts

Development has not been confined to hulls alone. Until about 40 years ago, masts were almost always built of wood, normally the soft, springy and resilient pines such as Oregon (Douglas fir) and Sitka spruce. Racing yachts tended to have beautifully crafted, hollow, Sitka spruce spars (masts or booms).

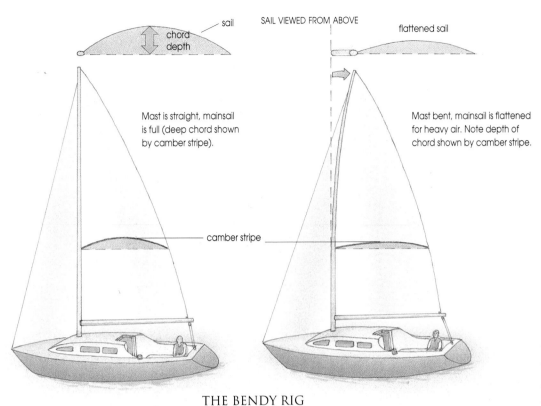

SAIL VIEWED FROM ABOVE

sail

chord depth

flattened sail

Mast is straight, mainsail is full (deep chord shown by camber stripe).

Mast bent, mainsail is flattened for heavy air. Note depth of chord shown by camber stripe.

camber stripe

THE BENDY RIG

Below *An Ultra 30 race boat with a bendy rig. This mast was probably set up with pre-bend, which can be increased by the on-board controls.*

From a racing point of view, the problem with timber was that it was not consistent. How fast the tree grew, how well the timber was seasoned, how the grain ran, these all played a part in the weight, flexibility and strength of the timber. This meant that masts built to identical specifications but from different batches of timber had different weights and characteristics. It definitely affected the performance of racing yachts – which need to be tuned to perfection.

In dinghies, spruce masts were perfected into the 'bendy rig'. This allowed the mast to be bent progressively as the wind strength increased, which flattened the mainsail. A flatter sail in turn increased the speed in heavy winds by depowering the mainsail and producing a better airfoil shape for the faster airflow. This was a breakthrough at the time and virtually signalled the end of reefing, or reducing sail, in racing dinghies. The mainsail was flattened, or 'bladed out', going upwind. Once round the windward mark when the mainsheet was eased, the mast straightened resulting in a full, powerful mainsail to drive the craft downwind.

A big breakthrough came in the late 1950s when aluminium masts started gaining in popularity.

Some custom-built aluminium masts had been seen over the years, but the changeover to aluminium was rapid. Aluminium was flexible, too, so the trend of bending the rig continued. The aluminium-alloy extrusions proved to be consistent, so masts with exactly the same performance characteristics could be reproduced time after time. This era saw the establishment of specialist mast manufacturers, which prevails to this day. (Previously, the boat builders themselves produced the masts for the craft they built.)

The bendy rig, pioneered in dinghies, soon spread to offshore boats, particularly from the late 1970s when fractioned rigs, until then almost universally used on dinghies, became popular again offshore. The aluminium masts adapted well to being bent on the upwind legs and straightened out downwind. The rigging to enable the mast bend to be properly controlled developed at the same time. Many offshore boats, not only those destined to race, now have facilities to bend their masts.

Carbon Fibre Masts

The next breakthrough came with the use of carbon fibre masts. For the foreseeable future, this development will probably be confined to top racing yachts and expensive cruisers, because it is exceptionally costly and requires complex production techniques. Where one of aluminium's advantages over wood was it's lightness for similar strength, carbon fibre was lighter still. This reduction of weight aloft increases stability, and thus sail-carrying ability. Coupled again with the ability to bend the mast, flatten the mainsail and depower the rig in a breeze, it has played a major role in increasing the speeds of the modern sailboat, particularly upwind.

SAILS

Sail Sheeting Angles

The closer the sails can be sheeted to the centreline, the closer the boat will point to the wind. But it is no good taking a full-sectioned, bluff-bowed cruising yacht, sheeting her sails close to the centreline, and expecting her to point high and sail efficiently. Very high pointing abilities are in general confined to high-performance racing boats with fine bows and easily driven hulls. The sheeting angles have only become closer to the

Above *A carbon fibre mast.*
Below *Sails made from Kevlar.*
Top right *Mylar sails on a Sigma 33 One Design.*

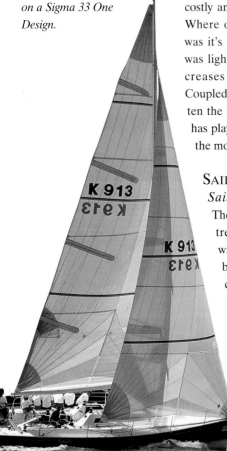
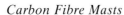

centreline over the years as efficiency of hull, rig and sails have improved.

Most serious racing boats have a traveller for their mainsheets, which allows an infinite number of different sheeting positions, including sheeting the mainsail to windward of the centreline in certain circumstances. The sheeting tracks for headsails have also moved steadily inboard over the years. This has improved the ability of the boats to point high, but has also increased the compression loads on the mast as spreaders have become shorter, and stay attachment points, or chain plates, have moved inboard.

Types of Sailcloth

While hulls, rigs and foils have been developing, so have fore and aft sails, mainsails and headsails. When you look at today's Dacron, Kevlar and Mylar sails, it is hard to believe that 40 years ago most sails were cotton. Compared to today's materials, cotton had many disadvantages. It stretched considerably – in fact, the sailmakers recommended stretching sails in light winds on sunny days before using them for racing. Cotton sails did not hold their shape for very long; they reacted to weather conditions – rain, and salt spray. If stored wet, they would rot and were damaged rapidly by ultraviolet rays (UV) from the sun.

Without doubt **Dacron**, a synthetic fibre, revolutionized the sailmaking industry and increased the performance of sailboats. Stretch was dramatically reduced, and since sailmakers no longer needed to allow for this, skills handed down for generations became obsolete. Sailmaking at that stage had still been something of an art. Shape was created by cutting the luff and foot in curves, while panels could be shaped individually. Optimum shapes were discovered by trial and error. Development was relatively slow as, little by little, sailmakers experimented by changing the shapes of their existing, fast sails. After the arrival of Dacron, sailmaking attracted many newcomers and, for a period during the '60s and '70s, some top dinghy sailors made their own race-winning sails at home.

Dacron not only produced faster sails. Shape was no longer influenced by the weather, and as a result of its resistance to rot, the sails could be stowed away wet, if necessary. The beautiful, creamy-coloured cotton sails were unfortunately gone forever.

Dacron also evolved even further. Stiffer cloths, with even less stretch, were produced for racing sails. They broke down more quickly than the more supple cloth used for cruising sails, but initially gave improved performance. On the whole, Dacron gave longer life both to racing and cruising sails.

After Dacron came the development of **Kevlar** and **Mylar**, the former again a synthetic fibre, the latter an extruded film, used normally in conjunction with a substrate to which it is laminated. Kevlar, particularly, stretches very little; however, it is prone to fatigue failure if it is flexed too much. Hybrid cloths, using combinations of Kevlar, Mylar and sometimes Dacron, have now evolved. Often referred to as 'brown sails' because of the colour of Kevlar, they are used on hi-tech racing yachts. Dacron is normally the choice for cruising yachts. **Nylon**, which has been around for a long time, is the ideal cloth for spinnakers. However, it stretches too much to be of use for mainsails and genoas (large triangular headsails).

As mentioned earlier, the role of more powerful and progressive computer programs played an important part in analyzing the stresses in sails under load. This led to different cloths being used in different parts of the sail. Different panel configurations were tried. No longer were most sails cut the same way, and the art of sailmaking became more of a science. Today's top sailmakers have computer-driven plotters which cut the cloth to exact tolerances; other techniques allow sails to be moulded to exact predetermined shapes.

Spinnakers

Sail development also proceeded apace with the cut and shape of spinnakers. These large, highly colourful sails (designed for sailing downwind) add considerably to the excitement of the sport, and can be difficult to set, fly and recover, particularly in heavy weather. Spinnakers are attached only by their three corners: the head and the two clews, or lower corners. Not restricted by being attached to a spar, or headstay, they can be difficult to control.

In the days of cotton sails, many spinnakers were asymmetrical in design. With the development of nylon and Dacron, the trend moved back to symmetrical spinnakers. There was still a tendency, lasting until about the mid-1970s, to

Above *Sail-making in progress.*
Left *A Fulmar Class yacht with Dacron sails.*
Below *A spinnaker trimmed to perfection on a reach.*

have different reaching and running spinnakers. Until that time, most offshore racing sailboats would have one flatter-cut spinnaker, often star-cut (the cut and orientation of the panels were laid out to resemble a star), in their inventory specifically for reaching.

As spinnakers improved in design and became more stable, more cloth could be worked into them, increasing their pulling power while still abiding by the regulations governing spinnaker size and shape. With the improved sail shapes, spinnakers that were previously efficient only for running could effectively be used for reaching.

However, nothing remains static: because of the great speed breakthroughs with skiff-type dinghies, sports boats, offshore multihulls and monohulls such as the Whitbread 60s, special reaching spinnakers were once again required. The extremely high speeds at which these craft travelled simply pushed the apparent wind so far forward that a need for a specially designed flat spinnaker was created. The

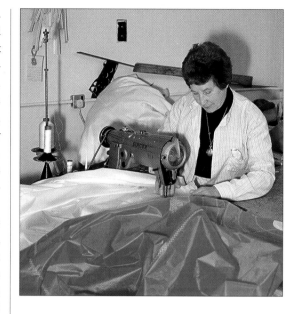

sail development race was on again, resulting in the modern asymmetric spinnaker, which has not yet attained the pinnacle of its potential.

Since the development of sailboat hulls and rigs has made modern boats so much more easier to control, spinnakers are now routinely carried under conditions that would have been simply unheard of some years ago.

As perfection cannot remain a permanent state, the development of hulls, rigs and sails will no doubt continue into the future, and their increased refinements will enable sailboats to become ever faster.

SAILBOAT GEAR

While the boats themselves have progressed, the development of the gear and fittings needed to handle the sailboats has not stood still. Much of the equipment commonplace today did not exist 20 years ago (this applies to both cruising and racing sailboats). Most of this gear is related to sail handling – no real surprise since it is the primary activity aboard a sailboat.

Roller Furler Headsails

Roller furler gear did exist earlier this century, but it tended to be somewhat unwieldy and seemed to disappear as the years progressed. Nonetheless, the principle of being able to furl a headsail by pulling a single rope was excellent, and the idea surfaced again many years later.

Top right *A spinnaker being sewed.*
Below *Foredeck activity during a round-the-buoys race.*

Improvements in materials and the engineering of the gear created highly efficient roller furling gear. Nowadays many cruisers carry this headsail gear as standard equipment. The sail is usually left on the forestay while the sailboat is in commission. A strip of special UV-protection cloth is sewn to the leech of the headsail, and this is all that can be seen when the sail is fully furled.

With the headsail fully unfurled, the sail shape is normally very good. An advantage, especially for cruising yachts, is that a number of intermediate headsails is no longer necessary, as the roller furler headsail can be reefed to represent various sized headsails by partially furling it. It normally does not set as well in the reefed situation as a purpose-made smaller headsail, but it creates considerably less work than does the changing of headsails.

While most racing craft do not favour this gear, it is invaluable in the single-handed racing craft such as the Open 60s.

Mainsail Reefing and Stowage Systems

For hundreds of years, reefing was done the same way – by the system of reef points. On a typical mainsail, the tack and clew were pulled down and secured, and a number of reef points tied in. The

points took part of the load, and tension had to be taken into account when tying each reef point, otherwise tears could result.

Then came a breakthrough: the roller reefing gooseneck was invented. By rotating a handle at the mast, the boom itself turned, taking up the unwanted sail area. This was an excellent system, requiring much less labour than the traditional system. However, it had one big drawback: as the mainsail was reefed further and further, it got progressively more baggy, or full – this at a time when, for optimum performance in high winds, a flatter mainsail was far more efficient.

The next development, known as jiffy reefing, was a great improvement on the old points reefing system. With the immense strength of modern sailcloths, it was found that properly constructed sails could withstand the forces of heavy winds by being anchored at the luff and clew alone. In crewed yachts, the sail could be rapidly reefed by hauling down the luff of the sail and hooking in the reef cringle at the tack, while the reefing line through the clew was winched down. The sail was now efficiently reefed and the excess cloth could be tidied up in a relatively leisurely fashion.

Left The headsail roller furler system is nowadays used by many cruising yachts.

SAILING TERMS

- **Spreaders**: struts (in pairs) to either side of mast; increase spread of shrouds and stays
- **Guy**: rope attaching end of spinnaker pole to boat
- **Warp**: rope used to moor, tow or anchor a vessel
- **Tack**: forward lower corner of a sail
- **Clew**: lower aft corner of a sail when the leech meets the foot
- **Luff**: leading (forward) sail edge
- **Leech**: aft (rear) edge of sail
- **Roach**: curved part of leech which extends outwards of an imaginary line between head and clew of mainsail
- **Reef points**: lashings to neaten up a jiffy-reefed sail
- **Reef cringle**: cringles in luff and leech of a sail which are pulled down to form reefed sail
- **Single-line reefing**: involves pulling a single piece of rope
- **Stemhead**: the fitting at deck level at the bow of a boat

Left A headsail furled by the roller furler method.

Above *A mainsail furled on an in-mast furling and reefing system.*
Below *A boat equipped with an in-mast reefing system*
Right *A billowing gennaker.*

Shaking out the reefs is quick and easy, while jiffy reefing results in a well-set sail, so important for racing. These days, most offshore racing yachts have jiffy reefing systems.

Many cruising yachts have variants of jiffy reefing, such as single-line reefing. Here the reefing line is rigged in such a way that by winching it, the luff and leech pull down simultaneously. Not quite as fast as the system used for racing, it is however very good for short-handed cruisers.

In-Boom and In-Mast Systems

There are two expensive, but effective, systems for cruising yachts which not only make reefing easier, but, like a roller furler headsail system, take care of the stowage requirements as well.

The in-mast reefing and stowage system rolls the mainsail up inside the mast. Some sacrifices are made; for example, most of the mainsails used for this system do not have battens, which reduces the sail area (there is no roach) and detracts from the set of the sail. This problem is being addressed, and both vertical batten and very flexible horizontal batten systems are being developed.

A rarer variation is the in-boom reefing system where the mainsail is rolled up inside a specially constructed boom. The sail can be hoisted and set at any position to provide exactly the sail area required. The set is not quite as good as a conventional mainsail, but is quite acceptable for fast, easy cruising.

Spinnaker Snuffers

The spinnaker can be a difficult sail to control, so is often not a favourite of cruising sailors. The snuffer, a sock-like device which encloses the spinnaker, can be used to simplify hoisting, setting and retrieving the spinnaker. In its retracted position, the snuffer remains just above the spinnaker head; when the spinnaker is collapsed by easing the guy (a rope running from the boat to the end of the spinnaker pole) and the sheet (controlling the spinnaker), the snuffer is hauled down by a rope tackle, encasing the spinnaker.

Gennaker

The gennaker is a sail that has been developed for cruising sailors who do not want the problems of a spinnaker but who would at times like additional speed. A cross between a spinnaker and a genoa, it does not require a spinnaker pole. The sail is tacked down to the stemhead, but is hoisted flying (not attached to a headstay). It is easier to control than a spinnaker, its major disadvantage being that without a pole, it can only be used on a reach to approaching a broad reach. On a run, it simply collapses.

Fully Battened Mainsails

You only have to look at the Chinese junks to confirm that fully battened sails have been around for a long time – and in recent times they have again become popular. From a cruising point of view, full-length battens produce a mainsail that does not flap violently, and is therefore docile and easy to handle.

For the racing sailor, a fully battened mainsail has all of these advantages, but also the fact that the battens can contribute to controlling sail shape, and to holding out a large rounded roach, thus allowing considerably more sail area.

Winches

Winches have steadily improved over the years (*see illustration on page 64*). Around 50 years ago, most winches were of the bottom-handle type. The travel of the winch handle was restricted – it could not be rotated through 360 degrees, and it was operated in a jerky to-and-fro movement. Then came top-handle winches, where the winch handle fitted into a recess in the centre of the winch and could revolve a full 360 degrees. This great improvement allowed the operator to assume a much more effective position.

With the winches, continued development of their bearings and life expectancy also improved, but the biggest breakthrough was the geared winch. Low gear in many winches was simply engaged by rotating the handle in the opposite direction, or by pushing a button.

The next step was the invention of the self-tailing device, whereby the need for a tailer, holding the sheet or halyard while another person operated the winch, was eliminated. Self-tailing winches were a boon to cruiser and racer alike, and nowadays are fitted to most sailboats.

Below left A fully battened mainsail on a 38ft (12m) Tortarolo 38-design boat.
Below Jammers and self-tailing winches.
Inset A happy genoa trimmer! The winch shown is a self-tailer, but the self-tailing device is not in use here.

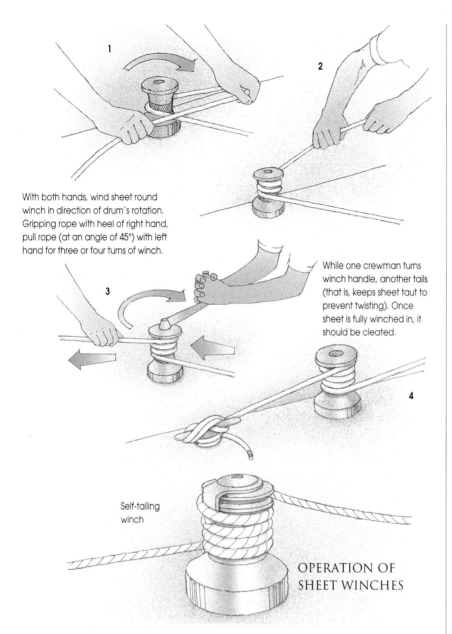

With both hands, wind sheet round winch in direction of drum's rotation. Gripping rope with heel of right hand, pull rope (at an angle of 45°) with left hand for three or four turns of winch.

While one crewman turns winch handle, another tails (that is, keeps sheet taut to prevent twisting). Once sheet is fully winched in, it should be cleated.

Self-tailing winch

OPERATION OF
SHEET WINCHES

Above right *An impressive array of boat winches laid out on a single-handed racing yacht.*
Right *An adjustable genoa car.*
Following pages *Nicorette, a modern racing Maxi, winner of the 1995 Fastnet held in the UK.*

Roller Bearing Blocks

Roller bearings make a great difference to the efficiency of blocks, or pulleys, and certainly most of the blocks fitted to racing sailboats these days are the roller bearing type. The only servicing necessary on most brands is a rinse in fresh water.

Adjustable Genoa Cars (Slides)

Genoa cars on keelboats and offshore racers need to be adjusted often, and although there have always been adjustable cars, one has to take the pressure off them to enable one to pull up the holding pin, slide the car to its new position and re-engage the pin. Nowadays, on racing sailboats at any rate, roller bearing headsail cars, adjusted by a rope tackle, are almost standard. They can be moved under load, and are used in racing as part of the regular trimming mechanisms for headsails. Moving the car aft opens the leech and depowers the headsail in gusts of wind, while moving it forward has the opposite effect. Being able to move these cars under heavy load is possible mostly due to the efficiency of roller bearings.

Mainsheet Travellers

Mainsheet travellers play a very important part in mainsheet trim. Starting off as extremely simple devices, most travellers today are based on roller bearing systems and are easily adjustable by the helmsman or the mainsheet trimmer. Many travellers are operated by a block-and-tackle system that's accessible to the helmsman or trimmer.

Below *Ropes and traveller on a Flying Dutchman Class boat.*
Bottom left *A selection of three-strand and plaited synthetic ropes, colour-coded.*
Bottom *Sheets and guys drying on the pulpit.*

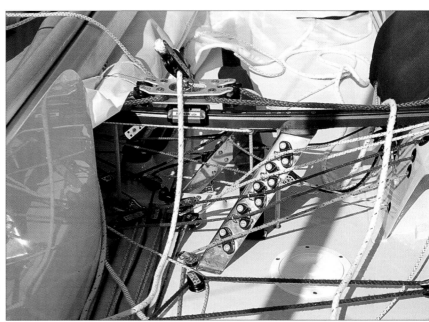

Rope

Rope has not escaped development. Without doubt, today's synthetic fibre ropes are very much stronger and longer lasting than their natural fibre counterparts of some years ago. They have the same advantage as today's sails – in the event of being stowed wet, they will not rot.

New fibres on the market, such as Kevlar and Spectra, have reduced stretch and increased the strength of modern ropes. Some stretch is advantageous in anchor rodes (or warps), and nylon is an excellent material for these. Fortunately, the traditional knots (*see* Chapter Nine) all work well with the synthetic fibres, but splicing techniques are often very different.

CHAPTER FIVE

TYPES OF SAILING

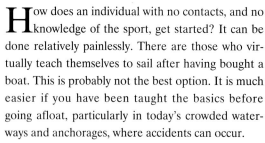

How does an individual with no contacts, and no knowledge of the sport, get started? It can be done relatively painlessly. There are those who virtually teach themselves to sail after having bought a boat. This is probably not the best option. It is much easier if you have been taught the basics before going afloat, particularly in today's crowded waterways and anchorages, where accidents can occur.

The best way is to join a sailing club, or enrol in a course at a sailing school. Many reputable sailing schools operate around the world, and most provide an excellent grounding. Some train in dinghies while others specialize in keelboats. Sailing clubs are always on the lookout for new members and are usually happy to assist newcomers to find crewing positions; they give good advice on obtaining the right sort of boat.

DINGHY SAILING

Dinghies are an excellent way to start sailing after having learnt the basics. Provided you are not after an expensive racing machine such as a 49er or a 505, dinghies are available at reasonable prices, and are very suitable for practising the rudiments of sailing.

Because most dinghies are extremely responsive, and their crews are close to the water, dinghy sailors on the whole understand their boats and the water well. Those who race learn very quickly how to trim their boats, how hard to sheet the sails, and where to place their weight to get optimum performance.

Dinghies are almost all centreboarders and, with the boards partially raised, can sail in fairly shallow water, opening up endless sailing possibilities in a variety of locations. One of their attractions is that

Above *A Hobie 14 on a reach.*

The Hamble River Dinghy Sailing School, Southampton (UK), at work.

they can be sailed in many different areas, due to their portability. A large number of people are happy just cruising dinghies in peaceful surroundings, while others use them for serious racing or as a stepping stone for sailing aboard keelboats. A dinghy can be towed on a road trailer by a reasonably sized family saloon car, and smaller ones can be carried on the roof of the car.

Dinghy sailing not only brings you close to nature and the beauty of your surroundings, it also encourages an understanding of weather and tides (*see* Chapter Two). This is an important safety aspect, and an awareness of it is essential when racing. The person who sails his boat fast is not always the winner. Knowledge of strategy, weather and tides plays a major role.

There are many facets to sailing, allowing something to suit everyone. Even if you are never going to be a top crewman on an ocean racer, there is a place in the sailing world for you!

While sailing dinghies is an excellent way to begin (and many top offshore sailors often recruit dinghy sailors as crew and helmsmen), it is not the only way to initiate one's interest. Some people enter the sailing world at an age when they may feel dinghy sailing is too athletic for them. A good starting point is to take a course with a school specializing in keelboats or to join a keelboat club.

In the immediate post-war era of the sailing explosion (covered in Chapter One: A Historical Overview), most dinghies were built of wood – many by the owners themselves. The joinery work was often exquisite. Varnish – or a combination of varnish and high-gloss paint – was generally the finishing medium.

A big part of having a dinghy, too, was pride of ownership – and for the owner of a home-built dinghy, the satisfaction of having created a practical thing of beauty was that much greater!

Unfortunately, in today's world of the 'pop-out' fibreglass dinghy, few amateurs still construct their own boats. Some of the pride of ownership has perhaps been lost in the process; on the other hand, the modern fibreglass or composite boats need little maintenance. In suitable climates, or where winter 'frostbite' events are held, these boats can be sailed throughout the year. The long months of annual maintenance required by the wooden boats are a thing of the past.

Dinghies can be sailed virtually anywhere there is water. We find them active on rivers, inland bodies of water such as lakes and dams, commercial harbours, lagoons and also off the beaches – the famous Hobie Cat catamaran in its 14ft (4.2m) and 16ft (4.8m) versions originated as an 'off-the-beach' boat. Both have successfully served in this role for several decades. The Hobies are an excellent example of boats that have a racing following, but are also used by a strong contingent of sailors for leisure sailing only.

Mankind has always been competitive, as history so clearly shows, so racing will continually be a very important part of sailing. Most sailors, whether they are amateurs or professionals, will at some stage in their sailing careers engage in some form of racing.

DINGHY RACING

Dinghy racing is an excellent medium to test skills and ability. Most popular classes have fleets racing at main venues in their country of origin, or world-wide in the case of international classes.

The most popular classes are the one-designs with their equality in performance, thereby allowing the most skilful crew to win. The rules, particularly in the less specialized classes, do away with the 'cheque book race' by prohibiting the use of exotic and expensive equipment. Sensible restrictions are placed on the materials used to build the craft and the cloth used for sails. This helps to ensure that boats in a specific class are of a similar speed and a reasonable cost.

There are often large numbers of one-design dinghies in a race, and therefore very close racing ensues. Changes usually happen quite fast in dinghy racing, and you will soon gain some experience in tactics and become familiar with the racing rules. Racing against other identical boats immediately highlights those that are going faster, and you can experiment easily to find out why this is the case. Is the mainsail perhaps sheeted in too hard? Is there less current up against the sandbank? These and numerous other questions pose themselves time and time again. For the newcomer to sailing, dinghy racing has a steep learning curve and provides an excellent base for any other type of sailing which may follow in the future.

Above *Optimists taking part in a race.*
Opposite *Racing in Mirror dinghies – one of the most popular (and numerous) 'DIY' Class boats designed.*

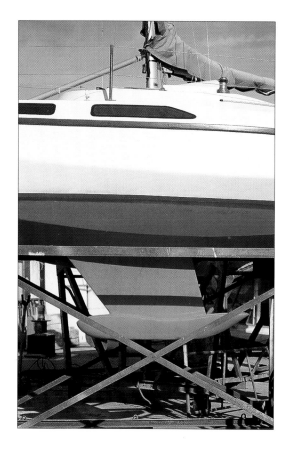

Above *On the hard for routine maintenance. This picture clearly shows the keel and the ballast at its base.*
Above right *A Dragon Class day racing keelboat.*
Right *Typical small keelboat.*

KEELBOATS

While some make dinghy sailing their main activity, others move on to keelboats or offshore racers. The popular small keelboat classes are usually crewed by two, three, or perhaps four people and are essentially day boats (that is, they have no accommodation). Because they have fixed keels, their activities are limited to deeper water, and they are usually found on lakes or in suitable places along the coastlines of the world. Again, many of these keelboats are one-designs, and very close racing can be expected.

Skills learnt racing dinghies stand you in good stead for racing keelboats. They are of course heavier, they carry more way (that is, carry on moving when the wind drops or sails are lowered) and can cause more damage than a dinghy in the event of a collision. After perhaps some initial nervousness, a dinghy sailor will quickly become adept at handling keelboats and will soon learn to get the best out of them. The important thing is that they respond to exactly the same techniques as dinghies do. The smaller keelboats almost always compete in day races, which are sailed 'around the buoys'.

OFFSHORE RACING

Although offshore racers are usually bigger than the keelboats just described – and are fitted with bunks, a navigation station, galley and auxiliary motor – they often do most of their racing around the buoys. Again, the same skills required to sail dinghies well are required here. Offshore racing yachts do participate in offshore passage races, and club-level offshore racers or cruisers/racers are regularly used too for cruising.

For both racing and cruising offshore, a whole host of new skills is required over and above the basic ability to sail the boat. The gear on offshore sailboats is considerably heavier and can cause injury to people who are not aware of the potential dangers.

You can commence offshore racing by joining a good crew, even if you have little basic sailing knowledge yourself. The opportunity to join such a

crew, watch them in action and do odd jobs as instructed is a good way to gain this knowledge.

Once you are off on a long-distance race, probably finishing in another port, you have to know where you are. Navigation becomes an important factor. Today, with the Global Positioning System (GPS) (*see* page 93) based on satellites, which is almost standard on seagoing sailboats, it is easy to plot a position accurately at any time and in any weather. The ability to plot an accurate position does not, however, eliminate the necessity to account for tidal streams, currents, obstructions and the like; GPS simply allows you to devote more time to other areas related to safe and effective navigation.

Secondly, a good knowledge of weather systems and how they work is essential (*see* page 28–31). There are many weather forecasts available. Some craft are able to receive synoptic charts by weather-fax equipment on board – transmissions are at

Above *The navigation station on a yacht.*
Below Orion Express *at the start of an offshore regatta (Corum Cup) in Hong Kong.*

preset times. The results of a race, and in fact the safety of the craft, can hinge on the correct interpretation of the data available, and the weather signs themselves. Cloud formations, temperature, the state of the sea, and that basic and reliable tool, the barometer, all tell a story and give valuable pointers.

Nowadays most small seagoing craft carry radios, or transceivers (*see* page 127). Very High Frequency (VHF) is a short-range, line-of-sight system, with a range of approximately 30 nautical miles. It is used universally around the world's coasts. The transceiver on board the craft must be licensed, while some countries insist that the set's operator also be licensed. The licence is relatively easy to obtain.

For ocean work, long-range radio comes into play and here Single Side Band (SSB) radio is used. The craft's installation as well as the operator must be licensed. This licence is usually slightly more difficult to obtain than that required for VHF.

Modern sailboats usually have a diesel auxiliary engine and numerous electronic devices, therefore it is imperative that someone on board the boat has a knowledge of these systems and some idea of how to keep them operating.

Some knowledge of first aid will also be necessary, and most seagoing sailboats will carry a well-equipped first-aid outfit. Food supplies and meals will have to be carefully planned and some of the crew will have to be able to cook.

The reason for mentioning the above requirements is not to scare the prospective offshore sailor away, but to illustrate the wide range of subjects on which some expertise is required for successful and safe offshore sailing. The owner or skipper does not have to be proficient in all of these – the responsibilities can be delegated among the crew. When a group is assembled to form an efficient crew, the diversity of talents is often surprising.

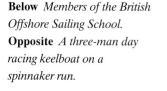

Below *Members of the British Offshore Sailing School.*
Opposite *A three-man day racing keelboat on a spinnaker run.*

Above *Leaving Malta at the start of the Middle Sea Race.*

Opposite left *Cruising in Barbados. Note the solar panels.*

Opposite right *A Finnish boat stops in at a port to relax and take care of maintenance.*

OCEAN RACING

For those competitive individuals who have the driving ambition as well as the means to race across the oceans of the world, this is a completely new scenario. To win, the boat must be driven 24 hours a day as if it were being sailed in a three-hour round-the-buoys race. The best sailing angles must be selected and the sails trimmed constantly. The weather needs to be monitored continually as weather systems definitely influence strategy and tactics. The ocean-racing yacht must be kept as light as possible; gear and equipment taken for granted by a cruising yacht is left ashore by the ocean racer.

There are classic ocean races such as the Sydney to Hobart, the Transpac from Los Angeles to Hawaii, and several others. For those really wanting to pit themselves against the elements, the BT (British Telecom) Challenge organized by Sir Chay Blyth takes a fleet of identical yachts the wrong way (against the wind) around the world, rounding Cape Horn in the process.

Another challenge is the Whitbread Round-the-World Race and, like the BT Challenge, is held every four years. The Whitbread has changed its format over the years and it is now a race for boats designed to the Whitbread 60 rule. They are very fast, very wet (their hulls are low and the waves sweep over them) and very exciting. The route takes the yachts south of the three famous capes: Cape of Good Hope (South Africa), Cape Leeuwin (Australia) and the famous – or infamous – Cape Horn (South America). To compete in a Whitbread, a sailor has to be physically fit and mentally tough. At the time of writing, these awesome boats have achieved 24-hour runs requiring an average boat speed of nearly 20 knots (20 nautical miles per hour), far faster than the famous tea clippers of the 1800s at their best.

Yet another hardy band of sailors tackles the single-handed race across the North Atlantic every four years. The boats develop each time, the sailors get better and whenever these events are sailed, records are broken.

CRUISING

What about ocean cruising, with its visions of idyllic surroundings and perfect weather? Perhaps that is what lures some ocean voyagers to cut their ties with the humdrum routine of life ashore and set off on a voyage of adventure. Of course, there will be those

unforgettable moments, sighting the tops of the palm trees on that low-lying atoll in the Pacific Ocean after a nonstop passage of thousands of miles; those spectacular sunsets so often seen at sea in the tropics; or the pleasure of a secluded anchorage after a hard passage. Long-distance cruising has its rewards. But, like most things worth doing, it requires a lot of planning, some hard work, some money and, occasionally, a little luck.

World voyaging really became popular from the 1950s onwards. Fortunately for those who want to take this up today, many books have been written on the subject. The best routes, the better seasons, the danger zones, are all well recorded.

Voyages can largely be planned before departure using information that is readily available. Provided you do not go into the world's particularly stormy areas such as the Roaring Forties in the southern hemisphere, or the North Atlantic in winter, it is possible for small inexpensive sailboats to make a round-the-world voyage, just as long as the various passages are undertaken at the correct time of year.

One of the most famous voyages in a small boat was that undertaken in 1959 by Canadian John Guzzwell. At the age of 29, he sailed his 21ft (6.4m) yawl *Trekka* around the world – beginning and ending in Vancouver. *Trekka* is now on permanent exhibition at Canada's Vancouver Maritime Museum.

Most people prefer a little more comfort than that offered by *Trekka*, and round-the-world cruising sailboats tend to be somewhat larger. You do not necessarily need a large, spacious sailboat with all the mod cons. There are a number of these around, but they are extremely expensive. For those who have to watch their chequebooks, simple boats, if properly designed and built, will get them safely across oceans.

A LIFETIME SPORT

Sailing is a sport which can cater for almost anyone's sailing desires. There is a place for those who just want to 'mess around in boats', those who want to sail tricky high-performance dinghies such as the 49er, and those who want to push Whitbread 60s to the limit in the Southern Ocean.

Depending on what you want to do, you either acquire the simple basic knowledge that allows you to enjoy sailing for pleasure, or pursue the in-depth knowledge of the expert in order to win sailboat races in competitive conditions.

One of the reasons for the allure of sailing is the fact that for many it is a lifetime sport. You can start quite young: eight is not an unusual age to commence sailing some of the excellent junior-class boats available in most countries. Later you can progress through dinghies to sail the most athletic ones such as the Olympic 49er between the ages of,

Left *Sailors preparing their boats before a race.*

Top centre *Topper racing with the UK Sailing Academy.*

Opposite top *An International 14 being sailed on a reach.*

Inset, far left *Bosun dinghy regatta (two-man crew).*

say, 20 and 35. You can then sail keelboats and the less athletic dinghy classes and still be helming an offshore racer in your 60s.

Another appealing factor is that the sport, whether it be racing or cruising, attracts women sailors as well. Women have proven to be competent cruising sailors, and excellent racing helmsmen and crews. Women have helmed or crewed in sailboats in most major events, including the Olympic Games.

Even the experts were novices once, so don't be afraid to start. Don't let the myriad different aspects of sailing disconcert you. Once you enrol at a sailing school, or join a club, or better still do both, you will be amazed at how quickly you learn. The nautical terms casually thrown about by the experts will soon become commonplace to you.

In order to be a good sailor, something to bear in mind from the beginning is that one should always try to be self-sufficient. Most sailing clubs have rescue launches, which operate when they are running races, while most countries have a Sea Rescue Institute or a Coastguard who is called out in cases of extreme emergency. The seamanlike way is to think ahead, anticipate problems, plan how to handle them, and try to get home without outside assistance if possible. Of course there are those situations where even the experts need help and the calling out of the rescue services is then justified.

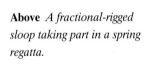

Above *A fractional-rigged sloop taking part in a spring regatta.*

Opposite bottom *Yachts are often associated with cruising in exotic faraway destinations.*

Left *Ultra 30 racing; this boat is skippered by British sailor, Laurie Smith.*

Committing yourself to voyaging in your own boat is a major undertaking. Without a doubt it disrupts your career, can affect the schooling of your children and a lot of your capital is tied up in the boat. Many sailors weigh up the alternatives and make the necessary sacrifices to cruise the oceans and visit new countries – and most never regret it.

However, there are many sailors who would like to cruise, see different countries and experience different cultures, but for various reasons will never be able to make the necessary break from their structured lives to cruise full time. For these people, bare-boat chartering could well be the answer.

Around 30 years ago the charter industry bordered on being amateurish. Often, charter boats were crewed by husband-and-wife teams on a world voyage, stopping off for a period of time to replenish the coffers. Now chartering is a big, well-controlled industry, and the opportunity for round-the-world sailors to indulge in part-time chartering is severely restricted.

Today, much of the chartering is termed 'bare boat', that is, you charter a fully equipped yacht, usually stocked up with food and fuel, but without crew. Charter times are up to the charterers; periods of a week, 10 days or two weeks seem to be the norm. Some very big reliable companies are involved – their names generally feature in yachting magazines.

The demands these charter companies have made in the yacht-building market are such that many boats have been designed exclusively for, or modified for, charter work. Normally, the resulting layouts would not be suitable for the long-distance cruiser, but are ideal for two, three or four couples to cruise for a few weeks within a few hundred miles of the charter company's base.

Charter companies exist all over the world these days. Areas such as the Mediterranean, the Caribbean, Mexico, Great Barrier Reef (Australia), parts of New Zealand, Seychelles, the UK, France, Tonga (Pacific) and many other places are home to well-run charter companies with excellent fleets of boats. All can be reached by air, and most charters could be fitted into a two- or three-week vacation, including travel to and fro.

For some, chartering is a way of 'testing the water' to ascertain if the way of life is going to be suitable for them. For others it is an enjoyable annual vacation and it is their way of experiencing other parts of the world and being able to indulge in their hobby at the same time.

Charter companies place reasonable, but not too onerous, requirements on charterers. They have to have a reasonable sailing background, but do not have to be acknowledged experts. Qualifications such as the yachtmaster series from your country's yachting authority, or a letter from your yacht club, are usually all that is required for proof of competence.

Right *A charter party.*
Top *Charter yachts under spinnakers and mainsails.*
Far right *A charter boat sailing in Maltese waters.*

The charter fleets often provide customers with an excellent way of ultimately owning a sea-going boat. Many of the well-established charter companies worldwide finance their craft via individuals who, after a fixed period of time (usually five years), take delivery of their craft after it has done duty in the charter fleet. Some of the charter firms offer deals along the following lines:

1. Put down 50% of the yacht's price and the balance is taken care of by the yacht's charter income. After the agreed period, probably five years, the yacht is yours.
2. Pay the full price of the yacht and over the five-year period you will receive a regular income which will amount to about two-thirds of the price paid by the end of the period.

During the five-year period the owner will not have to meet running costs, and will also be able to charter boats for himself from the company, worldwide, at very special prices. Charter boats are normally very well maintained and you can ultimately own a good boat.

CHAPTER SIX

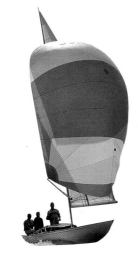

KEELBOAT AND COASTAL SAILING

GETTING ONTO THE WATER

Keelboats are easy to master if you have had dinghy sailing experience. For those who feel a little unsure of themselves and do not have sailing friends to show them the ropes, it would be a good idea to first take a short course at a sailing school.

Most sailboats which operate from marinas will have auxiliary engines – probably an inboard diesel or an outboard motor. Therefore most manoeuvring in the marina area will be under power, allowing one to go astern at the push of a lever. The boat will still be subject to wind (an important factor with a sailboat that has lots of windage – that is, the exposed part of the hull responsible for wind resistance), and the tide or the flow of a river. A good rule is to proceed very slowly in crowded marinas and anchorages. This has two major benefits: it keeps the wash (wake) low and therefore does not disturb other boat owners by violently rocking their boats; and if something goes wrong, you will probably be able to keep out of trouble by fending off (using your hands or legs to push off another craft), thereby not damaging your own and other people's craft. Good advice is to not come into a mooring

too fast under power, relying on reverse gear to stop you. If something goes wrong, damage could result. Rather nose in with enough way to maintain good steering ability, while a little touch astern from the motor will stop the boat. For early trips, while getting to know the craft, rather sail upwind of the harbour; it is then possible to put up the helm (alter course to bring the boat off the wind) and run home.

Top *Day racing Dragon Class keelboat.*

Above *Round-the-Island Race, Cowes, UK.*

Yachts under power and sail, manoeuvring slowly around a typical marina at Trinité in France.

LEAVING THE MOORING AREA

The golden rule of sailing, no matter what you sail, is to get a weather forecast before doing anything. Once this has been obtained and is satisfactory, check out the boat. Is the life belt in position, easy to deploy? Are there sufficient life jackets on board, and is there enough fuel for the motor? Do you have a simple first-aid kit and some distress flares?

Very important is drinking water: you can live for a long time without food, but fluid is essential. A small plastic jerry can of water should always be carried, even if you are only going for a short sail and have a six-pack of cold beer or a thermos of hot coffee aboard. A chart of the area is also important.

If you are sailing from a commercial harbour, make sure you know the rules. There are sure to be several in order to ensure the smooth operation of the harbour and to allow pleasure craft to coexist with commercial vessels. Familiarize yourself with these before setting out.

RULES OF THE ROAD

There are basic rules of the road which have to be obeyed. Those which apply all the time are the International Regulations for the Prevention of Collisions at Sea (IRPCS). These apply to both commercial and pleasure vessel activity, whether the vessels are propelled by power, sail or any other means. The only time that other rules apply is when sailboats are racing. The racing rules are based on the IRPCS rules but, in addition to the basics, cover activities such as starting, mark rounding and other complex situations. These are issued by the International Sailing Federation (ISAF) and are updated (if necessary) every four years.

Note that racing rules only apply to sailboats taking part in the race. If other craft come through the race area, the IRPCS prevail. The purpose of the rules, as their title makes clear, is to prevent collisions. It is worthwhile buying a copy of the IRPCS and familiarizing yourself with the most important ones.

Right of Way When two craft approach each other, one always has the right of way and the other must give way. The right-of-way vessel is known as the **stand-on vessel**, and the other as the **give-way vessel**. The basic rule for two approaching craft is: 'Power gives way to sail', the idea being that a power craft is more manoeuvrable than a sailing craft. However, there are exceptions: you cannot expect a large ship operating in restricted waters to keep clear of a small sailboat!

As the skipper of a sailing boat, you need to bear in mind the different IRPCS rules that apply according to whether you are under sail or power. For example, a sailboat under power, even if it has sails set, is still considered to be a power-driven craft under the IRPCS.

Many commercial harbours of the world have their own local rule which gives commercial shipping, including harbour craft and tugs, undisputed right of way. You must always make sure that you

MAJOR RULES OF THE ROAD

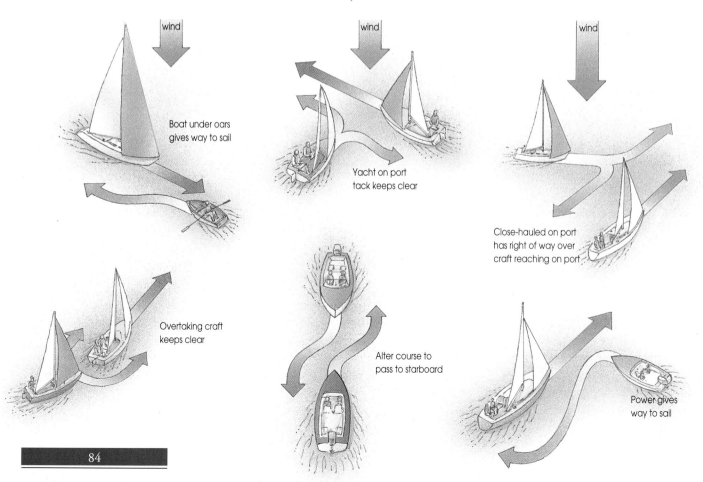

acknowledge this right of way. Never do anything that may cause the master or pilot of a vessel any concern. Make it absolutely clear that you are taking avoiding, or evasive, action. If you keep parallel to the commercial vessel, or make it clear that you will pass astern of it, you will earn the approval of the pilot or master.

Even in the open ocean where commercial ships are expected to keep clear of sailing vessels, they may be on autopilot (they have very few people on watch at any one time) and they also travel at speed. Between periods when the officer on duty looks around, or checks the radar, the ship could have travelled quite some distance. It is best to regard commercial shipping with respect, and keep well clear of ships if possible.

Keeping a Proper Lookout This is one of the most important rules, and one that makes single-handed long-distance racing so controversial. Technically, every skipper breaks this particular rule at some time in a single-handed race. It is vital to keep a lookout in a sailboat. While sitting at the helm on the windward or leeward sides, you do not have a clear all-round view. It is essential to keep asking crew members if all is clear in your blind zone, or to go and look for yourself at reasonably frequent intervals.

Two Craft under Sail If two sailing craft are in the same waters, the one on starboard tack (with the wind coming over the starboard side) has the right of way. If they are on the same tack, the windward boat must keep clear.

Overtaking Craft An overtaking craft must keep clear of the craft being overtaken. In the event of a sailing and a power craft needing to pass one another, and the craft under sail is the faster of the two, the sailing craft must keep clear of the power craft.

Sound Signals The sailboat skipper must be familiar with these signals. Although he will not often use them himself, the commercial vessels he meets will. One short blast on a ship's whistle means she is turning to starboard, two short blasts mean she is turning to port, while three short blasts mean her engines are running astern. Five short blasts mean, in short, 'Get out of the way!' It is a signal often given by a commercial vessel entering an area where there is heavy pleasure craft activity, or it may be directed at one vessel whose actions she does not understand but which is obliged to keep clear.

In a narrow channel, if a vessel coming up astern of a sailboat gives two long blasts followed by a short one, it means she intends to overtake on the starboard side. Two long blasts and two short in the same situation means she intends to overtake to port. Sailboats will not be expected to answer, but four blasts (one long, one short, one long and another short) mean, 'I understand and will hold my course'.

When two power-driven vessels approach each other head on, they should both alter course to starboard and pass port to port. If two power-driven vessels are crossing, the one which has the other on her starboard side must give way. In restricted channels, the basic rule is to keep to starboard.

A category of craft you are sure to meet is the fishing boat. These boats can be trawlers, drifters, long-line vessels or several other kinds. They are identified by specific shapes, or at night by their lights. Fishing vessels plying their trade carry out unexpected manoeuvres, so the best advice is to keep well clear of them.

In open water, when two craft are on converging courses, often at some distance from each other, it may not be easy to tell if a risk of collision exists. The easiest way is to take a series of bearings on the approaching craft with a hand-held compass. If the bearing remains constant, a collision may occur. Checking can be done very simply by using a stanchion with the observer standing in a fixed position. If the approaching craft's position does not change relative to the stanchion, there is risk of a collision.

Above *A sailboat on port tack clears a stationary naval vessel.*

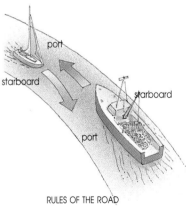

RULES OF THE ROAD
Sail gives way to larger powered vessels in a narrow channel.

NAVIGATION LIGHTS

1. Central white light = all-round masthead light for anchoring. Starboard = green. Port = red. Stern = white light. Under power = forrard white light.

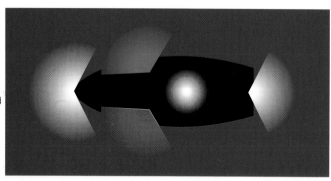

2. Small boats under 23ft (7m)

3. Under power: side, stern and steaming lights

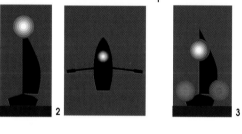
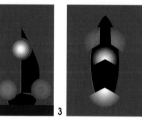

4. 23–65.5 ft (7–20m) under sail, side and stern lights

5. Under power: combined side lights, stern and steaming lights (combined or separate port/starboard lights optional)

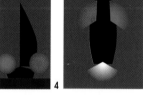
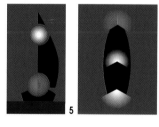

6. 23–65.5 ft (7–20m) under sail, tricolour light on masthead (optional to No. 4)

7. Under 39ft (12m) under power; side lights and all-round masthead light (or side lights, separate steaming and stern lights)

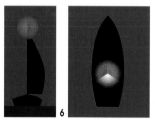
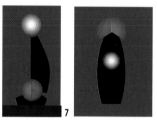

8. Power-driven (under 164ft; 50m)

9. Pilot vessel

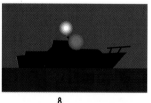
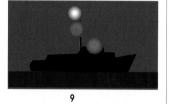

10. Large, power-driven vessel (over 164ft; 50m)

11. At anchor (all-round white light)

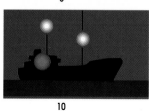
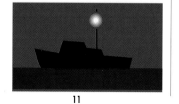

NAVIGATION LIGHTS

The configuration of navigation lights is spelt out in the IRPCS. At night, when other lights (such as cabin lights) are not visible – common in the case of sailboats – the navigation (or running) lights indicate the presence of a vessel. Their primary function is to indicate the direction in which the boat is travelling. The configuration of the lights indicates what type of vessel it is, and in the absence of white steaming lights, indicates that the craft is driven by sail.

Up until some 30 years ago, sailboat navigation lights were very poor in quality. Some excellent lenses were then developed in Europe, which intensified the light from a low-powered bulb without making it directional (early attempts only brightened the lights when seen from certain angles). Nowadays most sailboats that operate regularly at night are fitted with these lights; they far exceed the visibility requirements for sailboats specified in the IRPCS.

Sailboats are permitted several combinations of lights, however these combinations are not to be used together. A vessel under sail needs to show a port, starboard and stern light. These are often fitted

to the pulpit (railings at the bow) and pushpit (railings at the stern), about 24in (0.6m) above the deck. When the engine is being used, these lights – just above deck level – are switched on, together with a steaming light located above the other two that indicates the craft is under power. If the engine is switched off, this should also be the case with the steaming light.

Sailboats are also allowed to have a masthead tricolour light. It is most important to note that this light, which is a combination port, starboard and stern light using the power from one bulb, can only be used when the boat is under sail. As soon as the motor is switched on, the tricolour must be extinguished and the lower port, starboard and stern lights switched on. A steaming light visible under a tricolour is illegal. Many sailboat skippers use incorrect lights under power at night, confusing the professionals. While the tricolour is a wonderful light at sea and is visible in clear conditions for 4–5 nautical miles (8km), it is not ideal in harbours at night. Situated some 50–70ft (15–21m) above the deck, the light becomes lost in the background harbour lights, while the hull of the boat is difficult to see at water level. Use the lower lights when under sail in harbours and other well-lit areas.

Finally, the angles through which the lights are visible are clearly defined. Once a vessel has passed another craft, the port, starboard and steaming lights will no longer be visible. The vessel will then show a single stern light.

MAKING A COASTAL PASSAGE

In many parts of the world, there are numerous harbours, relatively close together, that are suitable for small craft. In such situations it is easy to make a coastal passage (to sail from one port to another). If there are any problems, one can stop at any convenient harbour. In other areas, however, there may be long distances between ports, with no sheltered bays in which to wait out bad weather.

Pilotage

This term refers to the navigating of a vessel in inshore (coastal) waters. Even on a hospitable coastline with a number of safe havens, one can always

get into trouble at sea. Plan a passage well, and never approach it with a cavalier attitude. Carry the right charts – for the area you intend to sail, plus extras of each side of your planned route. Things can go wrong and you may have to overshoot your destination. Small-scale charts of the coastline plus large-scale charts of harbours are essential. Most countries have chart agents who are qualified to correct and update charts. It is advisable to have charts checked before making a passage.

Above *Boats leaving the harbour in Lisbon, Portugal.* **Inset** *Navigation light and bulb.*

SAILING ACRONYMS	
CARD	Collision Avoidance Radar Device
CPR	Cardiopulmonary Resuscitation
DR	Dead Reckoning
EPIRB	Emergency Position Indicating Radio Beacon
GMDSS	Global Maritime Distress and Safety System
GPS	Global Positioning System
IALA	International Association of Lighthouse Authorities
IMS	International Measurement System
IOR	International Offshore Rule
IRPCS	International Regulations for the Prevention of Collisions at Sea
ISAF	International Sailing Federation
ORC	Offshore Racing Council
PHRF	Performance Handicap Racing Fleet
RDF	Radio Direction Finding
SSB	Single Side Band Radio
VHF	Very High Frequency Radio
VPP	Velocity Prediction Program

Opposite bottom right
A combination port and starboard light fixed to a fitting on the pulpit.

Above *At work in the navigation station.*
Right *The well-equipped steering position of a large sailing vessel.*
Below *A steering compass.*

Latitude and Longitude Lines of latitude and longitude are the universal measures of a specific position on the earth's surface. Lines of longitude run from the North to the South Pole, while lines of latitude run parallel to the equator. Every map or chart will represent an area on the earth's surface which is curved. Several methods can be used to enable the curve of the earth's surface to be represented as flat. One example of this is the Mercator Projection, a method used for many official naval charts (the earth is represented as flat). Degrees of longitude are shown on the scale at the top and bottom of the chart, while degrees of latitude are shown on the scale at the chart's left- and right-hand sides, thus forming a rectangular grid. Longitude is measured east and west of the Greenwich Meridian (0 degrees longitude), while latitude is measured north and south of the equator (0 degrees latitude).

Compasses For centuries, the magnetic compass has been the primary aid to steering and setting courses. In spite of all the modern development in electronics, it is still of paramount importance. It is recommended that you have your compass swung (*see* panel) to ascertain its deviation from the true course on different headings. If you have a pelorus (a device for taking accurate bearings related to the vessel's centreline) and possess the necessary knowledge, you can do this yourself, but normally you would get a professional to do it and have a deviation card issued. On most sailboats (except those made of steel and ferro cement which have mag-

netic qualities that affect the magnet of the compass), correction magnets are not necessary. Deviation may vary between 0 and 5 degrees, which is represented on the deviation card by an S-curve (*see* graph below right). You can check your compass by steering on a transit between two features marked on the chart, then checking the compass reading (allowing for variation) against the bearing given on the chart.

Deviation (caused by magnetism on the boat) should not be confused with variation (a result of the earth's magnetism). The latter is the difference between true north and magnetic north, and is measured in degrees east or west of true north. Variation changes constantly as your position on the earth's surface changes. In chartwork the compass deviation and the magnetic variation for the area must be taken into account. They must be conscientiously applied or significant course errors will be made.

If variation is west, add it to your true course to get magnetic course; if it is east, subtract. Draw yourself a diagram similar to the graph below and practise converting true courses to magnetic and vice versa. Use examples of east and west variation. An error in converting a true course to magnetic, with a variation of 20 degrees west, could result in a course that is 40 degrees off the intended one. Compass deviation also occurs east or west and is applied in the same manner as for variation.

As well as a steering compass, have a hand-held compass on board. Not only is it very useful to take bearings on buoys, lighthouses and conspicuous landmarks, it can also be used as a spare should anything happen to the main steering compass. It is also normally free of deviation, particularly if held well clear of the rigging (because of the magnetic pull in the metals).

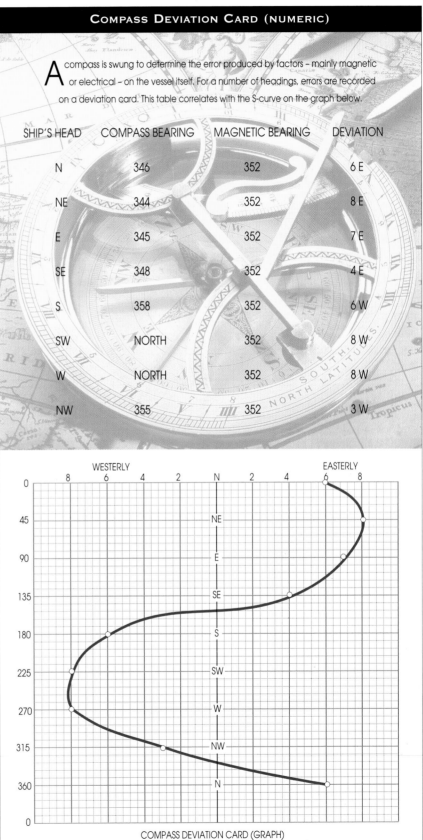

COMPASS DEVIATION CARD (NUMERIC)

A compass is swung to determine the error produced by factors – mainly magnetic or electrical – on the vessel itself. For a number of headings, errors are recorded on a deviation card. This table correlates with the S-curve on the graph below.

SHIP'S HEAD	COMPASS BEARING	MAGNETIC BEARING	DEVIATION
N	346	352	6 E
NE	344	352	8 E
E	345	352	7 E
SE	348	352	4 E
S	358	352	6 W
SW	NORTH	352	8 W
W	NORTH	352	8 W
NW	355	352	3 W

COMPASS DEVIATION CARD (GRAPH)

been written specifically for the small craft operator. Check with your chart agent or chandlery outlet for what is available.

Logbook Even if you are not going to write a descriptive log of your passages, do keep a logbook. Certain basic data should be entered, ideally every hour. Professionally produced logbooks are available. A good format is one blank page for individual comments, together with one ruled page with spaces for:

- time
- course ordered/made good
- distance travelled
- wind direction and strength
- barometer reading
- speed
- remarks.

At the top of the page there is normally a space for the boat's name, the passage being undertaken (from ... towards ...) and the date. At the bottom – more for use in ocean crossings – is space for the noon position, the run for a 24-hour period, and the run for the cruise to date. Engine and fuel usage can also be recorded here.

Above *General pilotage tools.*
Below *Wind direction and strength indicators.*
Below right *Logbook, charts and a pair of dividers.*

Basic Pilotage Tools

You need pencils, an eraser, a magnifying glass (useful to clarify some of the fine detail on charts), dividers, a set square and a parallel rule. Parallel rules, whatever type they are, can be somewhat difficult to operate on a chart which may be damp or have a prominent fold in it. This tends to render the parallel rules inaccurate. The 'roller' type of parallel rule is better, but there are a number of patent devices such as the Douglas Protractor, Portland Course Plotter and others, which help make chartwork easier.

For coastal pilotage, a reasonable pair of binoculars is probably essential. They are very useful for identifying landmarks, lighthouses and buoys.

Pilot Books

Pilot books exist for most ports of the world. They contain information on harbour signals, channel details, prominent landmarks, buoys, radio frequencies, port procedures, etc. Perhaps the best known is the formal-looking series of British Admiralty Pilot Books. Many books nowadays have

Game Plan or Strategy

Always have a plan for your passage. If the wind changes direction, what do you intend to do: put into another port, beat to windward or return home? If you are caught out in bad weather and cannot make a suitable port for shelter, what tactic should be employed?

Some countries insist on a simple passage plan, similar to an aircraft flight plan, being filed before pleasure craft sail on a passage. Points to be noted are: particulars of the craft, its safety gear, radio frequencies and – most important of all – crew list, next of kin and their addresses, together with the places the craft intends visiting and approximate arrival times. If these requirements do not apply in your area, do leave details with relatives or friends in case trouble does occur.

Bearings An easy way to fix your position if good landmarks (which are marked on the chart) are available, is to take bearings with a hand-held compass. Provided these bearings, when plotted, intersect as close to 90 degrees as possible, a good fix will result. A fix, known as a running fix, can be taken on a single landmark, over a period of time – generally an hour.

Buoyage Several buoyage systems are in use throughout the world (*see* page 92); each country, or area, selects a system to which all their buoyage should adhere. In addition, large-scale charts of harbours and the approaches to harbours normally show, besides the channels, individual buoys and their characteristics, such as colour and light sequence for night work.

Dead Reckoning (DR) The system of pilotage described earlier relies largely on visual aids to confirm your position. If you have to cover an area where land is not visible, or there are no prominent landmarks or buoys, such as a passage between two

headlands at each side of a very large bay or an indented piece of coastline, you can keep a good track of your course by plotting your Dead Reckoning (DR).

This is calculated by entering in the log the boat's distance run every hour, adjusted by allowances for leeway; favourable or adverse tides or currents; course changes and the like. From this information, a position – known as one's DR position – is worked out and then plotted on the chart.

When you get the feel for DR, it is amazing how close you can be to your true position after a considerable time has elapsed.

ELECTRONIC NAVIGATION AIDS

While the shore-based Decca and Loran systems have been available for years in certain parts of the world (they have become outdated as a result of satellite navigation), today's satellite systems are fairly recent. Satnav (satellite navigation) became available to small craft users in the mid-1980s. For sailors crossing oceans, this was an enormous boon; an accurate fixing of one's position could be obtained a number of times in a 24-hour period. However, Satnav has since become obsolete.

Above *A Bermuda-rigged ketch leaving harbour. Note the breakwater and navigation light.*

LATERAL BUOYAGE SYSTEMS

Zone A (as per the International Association of Lighthouse Authorities [IALA]) = Europe, most of Asia including India, Africa, and Australasia
Zone B = North, Central and South America, Japan, South Korea and Philippines

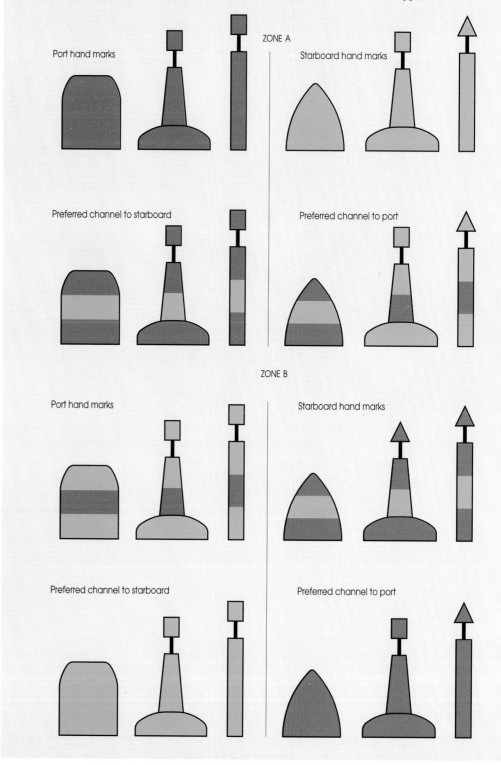

Global Positioning System (GPS)

By 1990 the Global Positioning System was available to small craft. GPS works on a system of orbiting satellites and gives a digital readout of current latitude and longitude. Initially the system was expensive and was used only on top ocean racers or cruising yachts. With the rapid development of GPS equipment for the leisure market, however, the cost fell rapidly, and a series of hand-held GPS units soon made their appearance. These perform a number of different functions.

The advantage of GPS is that it provides one's position on a continuous basis, and with the low cost of modern hand-held GPS's, most craft can afford to have one. Serious offshore cruisers and racers usually have a fixed GPS set at the navigation station, together with one or two hand-held backup sets. (This, you may think, almost makes pilotage superfluous, which is not a good train of thought! The controlling authority – it is a US system – has the power to switch off the service; and in rare cases, GPS's can go wrong.) It does make good sense to take along a GPS as it works 24 hours a day, in rain, hail or fog; and it is very comforting that wherever you are, whatever the conditions, the GPS can be relied on to give an accurate fix of your position. However, it also pays to keep up your pilotage skills.

Two things must be borne in mind concerning this system. The first is that the accuracy of a GPS is downgraded deliberately by the controlling authority for commercial use so as to make it less useful for foreign military purposes; therefore, for commercial purposes it is accurate between about 492ft (150m) and 164ft (50m). The second point is that many charts are based on surveys done years ago when today's instrumentation and systems were not yet available. Thus many of the positions of prominent landmarks, islands and other features shown on charts can be out by some considerable distances, several hundred metres not being unusual! Just bear this in mind: GPS is excellent, but do not expect it to take you into your marina berth in dense fog.

As pilotage is under discussion here, not crossing oceans, comments have been confined to inexpensive hand-held GPSs. Most of them work off penlight batteries but, most importantly, also have attachments which enable them to work off a sailboat's 12V electrical system. They are a great asset on board any seagoing craft.

RDF (Radio Direction Finding)

For many years Radio Direction Finding (RDF) played quite an important role in pilotage and coastal navigation. Lighthouses and other prominent shore-based features had transmitters sending a series of signals on designated frequencies, which the RDF unit on vessels could home in on. If two of these were within range, and the bearings crossed at a reasonable angle, a fix could be obtained.

However, RDF was never particularly accurate, as various outside influences could bend the radio waves. The skill of the operator also affected the results obtained. GPS has rendered RDF virtually obsolete, and not many sailboats carry it these days.

Log Recording (Distance Run)

In pilotage, and indeed navigating across oceans, it is very important to know your distance run. In the days of sailing ships this was achieved by what was known as 'streaming the log line': dropping the line, which had knots tied into it at calculated distances, into the water behind the boat and counting the number of knots to run out in a certain time.

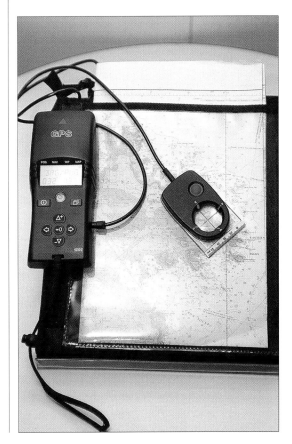

Above *A hand-held GPS.*
Left *The Yeoman navigation system allows GPS-derived positions to be plotted directly on a chart.*

Depth Sounder A depth sounder is an electrical instrument that measures the depth of the water by sending a signal to the bottom, which is recorded on its return. Not expensive, it is a most helpful aid to pilotage. An accurate knowledge of one's depth can be compared to depths shown on the chart, which in turn help confirm one's position. However, the normal depth sounder does not have a very great range; once the boat is far offshore, it is of little use.

A depth sounder can also be a great help with anchoring. Accurate knowledge of the depth gives you an idea of how much chain (or combination of chain and rope) to let out. Normally this would be a minimum of five times the depth of water.

Radar Many yachts are fitted with radar. The size of the units, as well as their power consumption, has dropped over the years, and they are now a feasible proposition in quite small craft. To be effective, the scanners must be mounted as high as possible.

Above *A satellite navigation monitor installed in a boat's navigation station.*

Then came the mechanical logs. A spinner was streamed on a line, and the line revolved, operating an instrument mounted on the stern of the craft. Called the Walker Log, it was used by generations of small-boat sailors. Only recently, in the last 30 years, have electronic logs taken over from the towed logs of the Walker type. Many small craft these days are fitted with an electronic log, all of which give the boat's speed in knots as well as the distance run.

A log is useful for good pilotage. Although you become fairly good at estimating a boat's speed, it is certainly useful to have your estimates confirmed.

Radar will detect other vessels, particularly those built of steel. It will also paint a picture of the shoreline and can be useful for navigation in coastal conditions. In addition, a radar device known as Collision Avoidance Radar Device (CARD) is available. This sounds an alarm when radar emissions are detected. It is a useful device, but only works when other vessels have their radar switched on.

Charts and Electronic Developments The paper chart is well known to most people, even non-sailors. The original British Admiralty charts, in use until fairly recently, were absolute gems. They made reference to the original surveyor and the vessel used, together with the date of the survey; sometimes this date was over 100 years earlier. Most, if not all, of these charts have now been modernized and although they are now crisp, clean and easy to use, some of the magic has perhaps been lost. One of the first breakthroughs since paper charts were

chart plotters, which have developed into today's electronic navigation centres. They display digitized electronic charts on which the yacht's position, usually acquired from GPS, is superimposed. Electronic charts are available for most parts of the world. The set can be the centre of the yacht's navigation system, and can be linked to wind and speed instruments, electronic compasses, and even radar. When linked to the boat's autopilot, it can also steer a course to the required destination. Like GPS, as these units develop, they are becoming less expensive and more user-friendly. This type of equipment is being fitted to more and more craft, but is not a substitute for conventional chartwork.

Weatherfax Most major maritime countries provide a weatherfax service. Faxes of actual and projected weather maps are sent at specific times of the day on nominated SSB frequencies. To receive these maps, you need a stand-alone weatherfax unit, or a printer which can be wired into the yacht's SSB transceiver. It is a great help to have these weather maps when crossing oceans, particularly when outside the trade-wind routes.

BUYING THE VESSEL
Dinghies are relatively inexpensive, they are easily bought and sold, easy to transport and can be stored at home. The decision to progress either to a keelboat of the day-sailer type, a small or larger sailboat capable of coastal cruising, or an even larger offshore boat, is a major one, however.

Above *A boat's autopilot equipment.*
Left *Steering compasses port and starboard, and electronic readouts for boat speed, log, wind speed and direction.*

Above *Dressed cruising yachts moored to a floating marina, or jetty.*

severe injuries or loss of life are involved, the repercussions on an individual's financial position could be far-reaching.

The legal system in some countries will permit you to get your crew members to sign a legal indemnity which will give the owner and skipper some protection in the event of an accident.

Moorings

The problems of finding the space in which to moor one's boat seem to mirror common problems that exist around the world – most of us, for instance, feel we pay too much income tax, regardless of our country of residence! Most sailing areas are short of mooring space, and it is important that you bear this in mind when buying a boat. If the boat is second-hand, ascertain first whether the mooring comes with it. Find out who owns the moorings, the mooring rights or the marina. Can the mooring be leased on a long- or short-term basis? If the mooring is of the swinging chain type, is the area protected from bad weather? Is there room for the boat to swing with the changing of the wind direction and the change in tides? Is there enough water to float the craft at

Survey

The investment is an even bigger step, and you need to protect your hard-earned money. If you are going to make an offer on the type of craft described on the previous page, it is a good idea to make the offer subject to a survey being carried out by a qualified marine surveyor. If his report indicates problem areas, the sale can either be cancelled, or the defects must be corrected before the sale goes through.

Of course, this does not apply to a new craft from the builder or agents, but the credentials of the builder should be checked. Ask yourself the questions: Are all their craft designed by qualified yacht designers? Do they hold their value in the used boat market? Have they got a good record for low maintenance costs? Are they financially sound?

Marine Insurance

Insurance will have to be considered. You may not bother to insure a relatively inexpensive sailing dinghy, but a keelboat is a different proposition. In addition to comprehensive insurance, consider third party cover (in many situations, this type of insurance is compulsory; marinas insist on it as do race organizers and yacht clubs). Major boating accidents are not that common, but when they do occur and

Right *Yachts at rest in the Royal Cape Yacht Club marina, Cape Town, South Africa.*

low tide? If not, is the boat suitable to take the ground at low tide (as many bilge keelers with twin bilge keels are)?

Before World War II, most sailboats swung on single chain moorings. With the subsequent boating explosion and the need to get many more boats into the same water space, marinas have developed in most parts of the sailing world. They tend to comprise a central spine, with pontoons (fingers) coming off the spine at right angles. Boats are moored on each side of the pontoons, and the whole system is designed to rise and fall with the tide.

Marinas vary considerably in price, depending on the location and the facilities offered. Some marinas have mooring facilities only, while others may in addition provide water and electricity; some may have a fuel dock, others small shopping facilities and perhaps a haul-out area. If you can afford it, a berth at a good marina is probably the best bet today. A marina also normally offers some security, as access is controlled.

A chain mooring in a pleasant waterway is a delight, but it has many drawbacks in today's fast-moving world. Firstly, the boat almost always has to

be reached by a small dinghy or by a ferry service. Friends and family cannot visit as easily as they can at a marina, and working on your craft is that much more difficult. However, chain moorings are considerably less expensive, and should not be ruled out, particularly if the budget is tight.

Registration

A sailboat will normally have to be registered, or licensed, in some way. It is usually a fairly simple procedure – the manager of the marina, or the local yacht club, will almost certainly be able to advise.

Should you intend to race the craft, there will probably be a little more paperwork. If you have selected a one-design, it will be necessary to join the association run by that one-design class. Also, a one-design should have a certificate confirming that it complies with the class rules; this will have to be transferred into the new owner's name. If the craft is of the cruiser or cruiser-racer type, it probably races in the local Performance Handicap Racing Fleet system (PHRF). If the boat is more sophisticated it may be rated by one of the many rules in operation around the world. Make sure the certificate is valid and have it transferred into your own name.

Above *Lymington yacht haven, Hants, UK.*

Following pages *At the False Bay Yacht Club's 1998 Spring Regatta in Cape Town, the Merlin, a Simonis 65, is on a close reach with the crew using their weight on the weather rail to reduce heeling and add speed.*

CHAPTER SEVEN

ADVANCED SAILING SKILLS

M any sailors, having reached a certain level, will be happy to remain at this level and sail for pleasure. Others may want to improve their skills and compete in club races, or in higher competitions. Yet others may simply wish to cruise, but also be able to set their sails efficiently and get the most out of their boats. This chapter covers some of the points which can help sailors attain good boat speed, and also looks at boat handling and some basic racing tactics. There are many books on the subject for those who wish to learn more.

While there are certainly some pointers to be given which will help you to sail more efficiently, it is still something of a 'seat of the pants' affair. There are some people who will never be top racing helmsmen, but they can enjoy sailing nonetheless. Once the basic skills have been mastered, they can easily be transferred to other types of boats, from dinghies to ocean racers.

BOAT SPEED

The term 'boat speed' says it all. That is what the top racing crews are striving for. Tactics may help you win races, but without good boat speed, consis-

tently good results are difficult to achieve. Even when making a passage, trimming your boat efficiently could have a result of hours, or even days, being shaved off the length of the trip.

While there are basic methods of achieving good boat speed, which are listed below, plenty of instinct is involved. Conditions may at first glance appear to be identical to those experienced before, yet the

Above *A modern offshore racer under full mainsail and 'blade' jib.*

An offshore racer participating in the 1991 Fastnet Race in the UK.

same trimming tactics being applied to the boat do not produce the speed. Something is often different: wind speed could be up or down a knot or two, or the tide against the wind could be producing a slight chop which requires more power to punch through. It is all these intangibles which make sailing such a fascinating sport, both for the top sailor and those who simply wish to enjoy the water.

Light Airs

The following is a list of pointers geared towards obtaining boat speed in light wind conditions while sailing upwind:

- very little, if any, mast bend
- main halyard tension not too hard
- mainsail foot tension not too hard
- no Cunningham tension

- not too much tension on boom vang
- do not oversheet headsail
- do not sheet mainsail in too hard
- start with mainsheet traveller in the centre
- do not point too high; it is easy to stall the boat in light weather
- watch the Windex, the telltales and the water to windward
- keep the boat moving
- consider heeling the boat to leeward to help keep the sails full and counter lee helm.

Moderate Breezes

As the wind increases, the trim is altered to make maximum use of the available breeze. The loose, almost baggy aspect of the rig, which is fast in light weather, will not be fast in moderate winds, upwind. Taking the following steps may help you:

- bend the mast moderately
- fully hoist the mainsail to the upper black band
- haul out the mainsail foot close to, or to, the boom end black band
- consider pulling down the Cunningham cringle to increase mainsail luff tension

Top *Light airs at the beginning of a race.*
Above *Racing on the downwind leg with spinnakers set.*

- pull in the boom vang quite hard
- sheet both the mainsail and the headsail harder than in lighter breezes
- keep the mainsheet traveller at or near the centreline – experiment with easing it a little
- if waves have not yet built up, point fairly high; as the chop builds up, it may be necessary to sail slightly freer to power through the choppy sea
- watch the telltales on main and jib; keep the weather telltale on the jib close to the point where it begins to lift
- the boat may begin to get a little weather helm – sail it as flat (level) as possible.

Heavy Winds

Many sailors get their boats going well in light to moderate winds. Those that master heavy air sailing often win more races in a season, or over a series – they are often better placed on overall positions. The points below refer to upwind sailing:

- bend the mast to its maximum heavy wind bend position
- haul Cunningham down hard
- keep the boom vang tight
- drop the main traveller to leeward to help de-power the mainsail
- keep the boat as level as possible – this is faster and helps relieve weather helm
- consider moving headsail sheeting position aft to open the leech and depower the rig
- watch for the correct wind strength to reef the mainsail and/or change to a smaller headsail
- in smooth water, high pointing is possible; in rougher water, sail freer
- hike out (lean out with feet secured by toestraps) fully in a dinghy, with crew on the weather rail in a keelboat.

Downwind Sailing

Sailing downwind requires different techniques to those used for upwind sailing. Almost all adjustable features can be eased out in all wind strengths. When pulling off, or bearing away to a point of sailing between a beam and a broad reach, bear the following in mind:

- ease the backstay, and straighten the mast
- ease the Cunningham
- consider easing the main halyard and the main outhaul to make the sail fuller
- consider easing the boom vang a little
- ease the main and headsail sheets until the sails are properly trimmed
- reaching or broad reaching in heavy winds, ease sails and pull off slightly in the gusts, head up a little in the lulls; the straightest course to the next mark is not necessarily the fastest. These manoeuvres can also apply to all wind strengths.

Downwind sailing is also dependent on what type of craft is being sailed. It may pay to sail some dinghies in nonplaning conditions, or displacement keelboats almost directly downwind. However, this will hardly ever be the fastest point of sail for the skiff-type dinghies, sports boats or fast multihulls. These are the boats that are so fast that they push the apparent wind far forward. It invariably pays to tack these boats downwind in a series of reaches.

Places can be made up by efficient downwind sailing. If you are going to race, it is worth paying a lot of attention to doing this well.

CREW DRILL

It almost goes without saying that crew drill plays a major role in obtaining maximum boat speed. Going through every manoeuvre is impractical in a book such as this – they vary from one boat type to another and also from skipper to skipper. However, some of the basics will be discussed. There are certain well-established methods of doing things in the various classes, or types, of sailboats. You could do a lot worse than watch how the top people in your class handle their boats and lay out their gear. Use this as a base.

Left Offshore racers sailing downwind.

GOING OUT ON A TRAPEZE

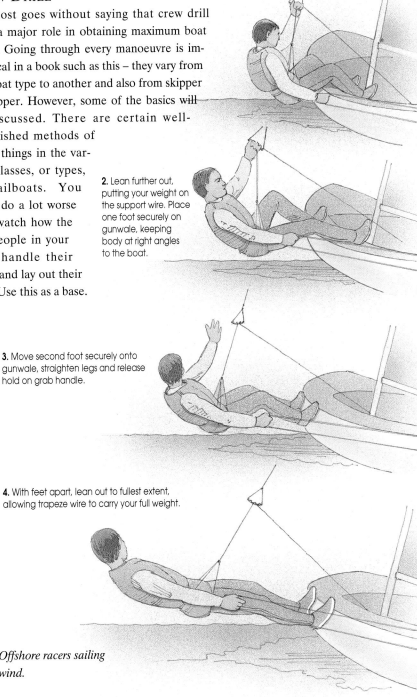

1. With feet secure in toe straps, hook trapeze into harness and sit well out on edge of boat. Hook hand in grab handle.

2. Lean further out, putting your weight on the support wire. Place one foot securely on gunwale, keeping body at right angles to the boat.

3. Move second foot securely onto gunwale, straighten legs and release hold on grab handle.

4. With feet apart, lean out to fullest extent, allowing trapeze wire to carry your full weight.

Above *Rounding a mark on the course.*

Going About

Going about, or tacking (*see* page 45), is a simple manoeuvre, yet done well, it can gain a boat length or two on competitors. Generally, the aim is to start the new tack with as much boat speed as possible, on the correct course, with the boat correctly trimmed.

- Start the tacking manoeuvre with a relatively small helm movement. As the luff of the headsail collapses, increase the helm angle (which increases the speed of the turn). At this stage the crewman lets go the headsail sheet (and makes sure it runs cleanly).

- At the conclusion of the tack, the helmsman must make sure the boat is on the correct course. Do not pull off too far. The headsail should be rapidly sheeted in, perhaps eased a fraction from the normal fully-in position, until maximum boat speed has been regained.

- In handling genoa jibs (usually on larger boats), make sure the genoa is not sheeted too soon – it could back (the sail catches the wind on the wrong side) and push the boat onto the original tack.

- Some boats respond to the mainsheet being eased very slightly after the tack. The sheet should then be pulled in steadily as boat speed is regained.

- In a breeze, crew movement must be fast. As the boat fills on the new tack, they must be hiking out, sitting on the weather rail, or trapezing.

Gybing

Gybing (changing course by allowing the wind to pass from one side of the sail to the other; *see* page 46) takes a little more consideration than tacking in anything but the lightest winds.

The traditional method of gybing while cruising is to pull in the mainsheet slowly, put up the helm, and then ease the mainsheet rapidly as the boom crosses the centreline. For racing in larger boats, this is nearly always considered too slow (except in strong-wind situations). Sometimes, if gybing in the middle of a leg, the skipper has some latitude in deciding when to execute a gybe. In this case you pick a good moment, for instance, as a gust eases off. However, if you are racing, particularly if surrounded by other boats, and you have to gybe around a mark of the course, you have no choice about when to gybe.

Most racing crews use the 'crash gybe' technique. If executed with care, it can be used on relatively large offshore boats, even in strong winds.

- To crash gybe, pick your moment (if you can). The skipper in a small dinghy, or perhaps a crewman in a larger boat, grasps the mainsheet between the blocks on the boom and the boat, i.e. if the mainsheet is a four-part tackle, he grasps all four sections of mainsheet. As the boat gybes the skipper/crewman pulls the boom across, making sure to let the mainsheet go as the boom crosses the centreline. Be very careful if you are going to crash gybe in heavy winds.

- There are many variations of this technique. For instance, it may not be possible to grasp the mainsheet in a small boat with boom-end sheeting. Here you may have to start hauling in the sheet to help start the boom coming across. Again, ease it the moment the boom crosses the centreline.

- If the boat has a mainsheet traveller system, secure it approximately on the centreline before a gybe.

- As the boom crosses the centreline, centralize the helm to avoid the boat rounding up. This is particularly important in strong winds.

- Never gybe with the boom vang fully slacked off – this could result in a Chinese gybe with the top half of the mainsail on the opposite side of the boat to the mainsail's bottom half (this was a regular occurrence before the universal use of vangs was commonplace).

Sail Handling

Just as crew drill in basic manoeuvres must be practised until it is close to flawless if you want to be successful in racing, sail handling must also be practised. To a good crew, it will be second nature.

Every sail handling manoeuvre must be swiftly executed, with the least disruption to boat speed (when racing, you need to remember always to think: boat speed). Adjustments to trim must be made rapidly with the least disturbance to the other crew members' concentration.

For instance, if the wind strength increases, the mainsail needs to be hauled tighter on the foot by the outhaul. Consider a fairly simple sailboat where mainsheet tension has to be eased before the outhaul can be tightened. Everything should be in place so that when the mainsheet is momentarily eased, the clew of the mainsail is rapidly outhauled to its new position, and the mainsheet hauled in again.

There are many different spinnaker handling systems. For the best system for your boat, check out how the top sailors in the class set up their boats. The most important thing is: whatever system you use, perfect your drill. The spinnaker must not only be rapidly hoisted at the correct time (mark rounding, for instance), it must rapidly be trimmed correctly and set perfectly. Places in racing can most definitely be gained in the hoisting, lowering and gybing of spinnakers.

Practice, practice and more practice is the way to perfect sail handling. Use the time available on the way out to the starting line to set the spinnaker, and also throw in a gybe or two. If the start is upwind, use the opportunity to sort out your upwind setup for the prevailing conditions.

Remember, even if you are not the hotshot in your class, your crew drill and sail handling can be perfected to match that of the top sailors. This may well be worth several places in a series.

Planning ahead is an excellent way to avoid surprises. If you sail a keelboat, get a crewman to watch boats ahead. Are the boats ahead able to carry a spinnaker on the next leg? Will it be a tight reach, or a broad reach? The answers will enable skipper and crew to think ahead and set the boat up in advance: the spinnaker pole preset to the correct position, and the mainsheet trimmer anticipating the correct trim for the sail. Taking all these factors into account trims seconds off your time round the course, seconds that are often crucial to a race.

Above and below
Bowman in action during spinnaker peeling (changing spinnakers without lowering one first).
Above left *Hanking a headsail onto the headstay prior to the start of a leg of the BT Challenge.*

Above *The Finnish boat* Vahide *taking part in the European championships for Swan Class yachts.* **Above right** *An offshore racer on a spinnaker run.*

Spinnaker Trim

Spinnakers have a mind of their own: apart from being large and full, they are only restrained by their three corners. They are therefore somewhat more temperamental than mainsails and headsails and it is more difficult to get the best out of them.

When reaching, they are fairly easy to understand. In a situation where the spinnaker pole is far forward for a reach – and practically parallel to the water – the spinnaker responds in a similar manner to a jib. Ease the sheet until the luff just begins to collapse or, if it's a modern spinnaker, begins to roll inwards. This is normally a fast trim (that is, setting the sail for maximum efficiency). Particularly when sailing in a one-design class with similar boats, experiment with pole height and pole distance from the forestay, and find out the fastest trim.

Different pole heights could be required for different sea states and different wind strengths. When sailing as close to the wind as possible under spinnaker, a header can cause the sail to collapse; not only must the trimmer haul in on the sheet, but

the helmsman can help by pulling off a few degrees. As has been mentioned before, the straightest course is not necessarily the fastest.

A particularly important secondary control on a spinnaker is the downhaul. This keeps the pole end from rising out of control. A sure way to initiate a broach in heavy weather is to let the pole end 'sky' (or rise up) suddenly. The guy, together with the sheet, is one of the primary controls. Not much trimming of the guy will be required on a reach but, once the boat is further off the wind, the guy could require constant trimming. On larger sailboats, it is usual to assign a crewman permanently to handle the guy.

As you sail further off the wind, the spinnaker pole is trimmed further aft, and the sheet is eased. The principal of trimming is still the same: ease the sheet until the luff curls. When the dead run is approached, the principle changes. Often the spinnaker collapses because it falls under the lee of the mainsail. Inexperienced trimmers may try to correct a collapse on the run by pulling in the sheet. This will compound the problem. In these circumstances the guy should be trimmed aft, squaring the pole, and the sheet eased. Only with practice do trimmers automatically recognize this changeover point.

The type of spinnaker discussed so far is the symmetrical sail, which has been developed to such an extent that it is far more stable and easier to set than its cousins of yesteryear. The modern fast skiffs and sports boats mostly carry asymmetrical spinnakers. These move the apparent wind so far forward that they rarely run anything like directly downwind. Asymmetrical spinnakers behave like larger, more powerful genoa jibs. They would never (except during a gybe) be blanketed by the mainsail as described above. As these fast boats reach downwind in a series of tacks, the asymmetrical spinnakers are generally sheeted in far closer than their symmetrical counterparts.

Striking, or handling, the spinnaker is another manoeuvre which, if executed properly, can gain you places in the race. If the spinnaker can be struck, or lowered rapidly, time after time regardless of wind strength, this is a tremendous advantage. Pick some buoys in your sailing area and practise rounding them, hoisting and striking your spinnaker. Practise gybing the spinnaker as well. If your boat handling and crew drill is excellent, you are well on your way to winning some races.

SAILING TERMS

- **Jib**: a triangular sail attached to forestay (set forward of the mast)
- **Spars**: a general term for booms, masts, yards, etc.
- **Spinnaker pole**: clipped at one end to mast, at other to spinnaker guy
- **Downhaul**: rope that hauls down a sail or pole i.e. spinnaker pole downhaul
- **Guy**: rope or wire that controls a spar, usually the spinnaker pole
- **Sheet**: rope attached to clew of a sail (or via a tackle to boom), used to trim sails
- **Clew**: lower aft corner of fore-and-aft sail where leech meets foot
- **Leech**: aft edge of fore-and-aft sail (symmetrical spinnaker has two leeches)

Top *Racing yachts running under spinnaker.* **Bottom** *The yacht* Reckless *drops her spinnaker while rounding the leeward mark.*

SIR ROBIN KNOX-JOHNSTON

Sir Robin Knox-Johnston must be one of the best-known and most experienced deep-sea sailors in the world today. He came to the attention of the sailing world in 1968/69 when he became the first man to sail around the world nonstop and single-handed in his 32ft (9,7m) ketch *Suhaili*. For this achievement he won the Golden Globe Trophy presented by the British newspaper *Sunday Times*. The voyage took him 10½ months. It is interesting to compare this time to that of the yachts taking part in the Jules Verne Trophy today. The trophy was originally meant for the first yacht to circumnavigate in under 80 days, thought to be impossible at the time. Nowadays circumnavigations are being achieved in just over 70 days.

After Knox-Johnston's successful voyage, sailed in a boat not really suitable for the trip but the only one he could afford and owned himself, came a series of sailing adventures. When his career as a merchant navy officer (he had his Master Mariner's certificate) came to an end, he achieved one success after another in the sailing world: line honours in the first Cape to Rio race (1971), honours in the Round Britain Race, sailing in the British Admiral's Cup team; these were just some of his achievements over the years. He sailed in both monohulls and multihulls, vessels that had one common trait – they were all fast!

One thing separates Knox-Johnston from some of the so-called 'boat jockeys': he is a true seaman, always considering the safety factors and never taking undue risks.

He hit the headlines again in 1994 when, together with New Zealand's Peter Blake, he co-skippered the giant catamaran, *Enza*, to a new Jules Verne trophy record of 74 days, 22 hours, 17 minutes and 22 seconds. During this voyage *Enza* achieved a 24-hour run of 520.8 nautical miles. She sailed 26,442.34 nautical miles at an average speed of 24.7 knots. With the speed of development these days, records do not generally endure that long. Quite soon after his feat, in 1995, Knox-Johnston's great rival, Frenchman Olivier de Kersuason, sailed a trimaran around the world in 71 days. Knox-Johnston is currently engaged in a giant catamaran project and hopes, with this new boat, to win back the Jules Verne Trophy.

STARTS

Most sailboat races commence at a starting line consisting of an imaginary line running between a buoy and a specified position on the start boat. In addition, apart from long-distance races where the start line may be specified well in advance regardless of wind direction, most round-the-buoy races are started upwind.

The fairest start line for the competitors is one which is at right angles to the wind, regardless of whether the first mark is exactly to windward or not. For one reason or another, it is not often that this ideal situation occurs. Start lines are normally biased, either to starboard or to port. This means that one end is a little (or, if the line is heavily biased, a lot) closer to the first mark.

The starting procedure is governed by the ISAF rules, and the start boat will be positioned on the starboard side of the start line, the buoy to port. The buoy end is often known as the pin end. Knowledgeable race officers will try and set a square line, or a line with a very slight port bias. Top competitors will always check the bias of a line and will tend to start from the favoured end, which in the case of a port-biased line is the buoy, or pin, end. This will keep the majority of the fleet from bulking up at the committee boat end, which can result in competitors colliding with the committee boat and each other.

A start line heavily biased to starboard is bad news. It invariably causes a large portion of the fleet to try and start at the favoured end, resulting in a chaos from which only a few craft may emerge with a reasonable start.

Why can the race officer not always set a square, or very slightly port biased, line? One of the reasons is that the wind is very rarely steady in any direction. It may be shifting slowly to the left or right, or it may be oscillating from left to right and back again. The time period between oscillations may or may not be consistent, and the number of degrees between the extreme left and extreme right limits of wind direction may or may not be consistent. If you have a compass (and you certainly should have), get to the starting area well in advance and check out the wind direction at suitable intervals (five-minute intervals is a good starting point). This can be done by heading the boat up to the head-to-wind position and then reading the compass, or by keeping the boat

Left *A fleet of French one-designs crosses the starting line of a race.*

close hauled and noting the change of course in degrees at set intervals.

To ascertain the bias of a start line, luff head-to-wind on the line itself. If the start boat is ahead of the beam, the line is starboard biased, and the reverse applies.

There are several starting procedures laid down in the ISAF rules. One aspect remains constant: sound signals will be given at 10 and 5 minutes before the start, and at the start. To make a good start, exact knowledge of the time is essential. There are many watches on the market that have been created specifically for sailors. Some skippers like the crew to call the time, leaving the skipper free to concentrate on the tactical issues in the hurly-burly of the start.

Where to Start

As far as possible, have a rough plan for your start. You do not know in advance what other boats are going to be doing, so you may have to modify your plan as the situation develops. Some factors to bear in mind are the following:

- Decide which end or where on the line you want to start.
- Start on starboard tack; you then have right of way over port tack boats.

- Decide which side of the course is going to pay – do you want to go out to the left-hand or right-hand sides or up the middle?
- Try to plan your start so that you begin with clear wind. If possible, avoid having someone on top of you blanketing you, or to leeward of you in the 'safe leeward' position (*see* page 110).
- If you believe the starboard side of the course will pay, start near the committee boat unless the line is heavily port biased. Try to create a gap astern of you so you can tack onto port soon after the start to get out to the right-hand side.
- It is no good starting in clear air if your boat is not moving at or near top speed on the gun. Being in a good position but dead in the water will invite competitors, who have started with way on, to sail over the top of you or through your lee. Aim to start with good boat speed.
- It is very important to get out of the start well. In those first minutes after the start, concentrate on boat speed – make the most of your start.

Below *Frenchwoman Isabelle Autissier, who has become famous for racing yachts single-handed around the world, in Cape Town for the BOC 1994.*

Some Basic Racing Situations

Covering

Every sailboat has a wind shadow extending to leeward of it. Another sailboat sailing in this wind shadow will have its speed impaired to some extent, depending on how close it is (*see* illustration below). This wind shadow effect plays a big role in sailboat racing. The well-known phenomenon of a tacking duel, where the windward yacht tacks every time the leeward yacht tacks, in order to keep her covered, illustrates the importance of wind shadow for legitimately hindering the opposition.

The concept of covering is easy to understand, but it must be executed well to work, especially when in close quarters with another (or other) boats. You may tack in the correct position to cover, but exit the tack with not enough way on, allowing the competitor to slip through your lee.

A good way to understand exactly what will or will not work with your boat is to go and practise with a friend in an equally matched sailboat. Try all the options and store the results in your mind for use during the race.

Keeping a Loose Cover

If your boat has managed to get ahead, the attacking boats astern start to dictate the tactics. Possibly you need to beat one of those behind you because of the points scoring of a series or for some other reason. Stay between that boat and the weather mark. Many a race, or series win, has been lost by not obeying that simple rule. This technique is known as 'keeping a loose cover' on a certain boat.

Close Cover

If you are fighting a very close race with a competitor, then you must apply a 'close cover'. On the beat, ensure that he remains in your wind shadow. Have your crew watch him intently so that the helmsman on your boat is given exact information in order to time his tacks perfectly. In close covering, a tacking mistake of a few seconds could cost a place, contrary to loose covering.

The Safe Leeward Position

Not quite as obvious and easy to understand as the wind shadow, the 'safe leeward position' also plays an important part in race tactics. Here, the boat a little ahead and slightly to leeward interferes with the one astern. The airstream, deflected from the windward side of the boat ahead and to leeward, has

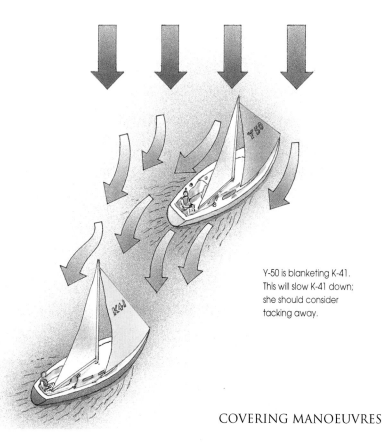

Y-50 is blanketing K-41. This will slow K-41 down; she should consider tacking away.

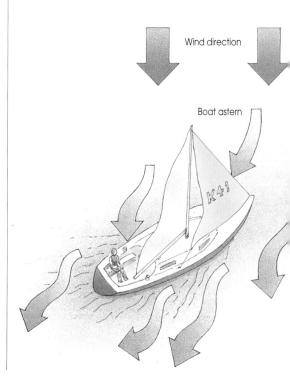

Wind direction

Boat astern

COVERING MANOEUVRES

Left *A close spinnaker reach for these racing yachts.*

a devastating effect on the airflow to the leeward side of the boat astern, with consequent deterioration in its performance.

Similarly with covering, in order to learn the exact effects of 'safe leewarding' the opposition, practise this manoeuvre with a friend in a similar boat.

There are many variables and conditions on the race course which are very rarely repeated exactly, so to win races you must have good boat speed and your tactics and strategy must be good. That is in part what makes sailboat racing a very absorbing and interesting pursuit.

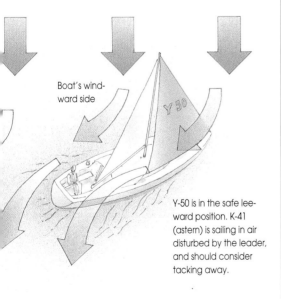

Boat's wind-ward side

Y-50 is in the safe lee-ward position. K-41 (astern) is sailing in air disturbed by the leader, and should consider tacking away.

SAFE LEEWARD POSITION

WIND SHIFTS

Wind shifts, or changes in direction, even if they are only a few degrees, can make a big difference to your position on the beat (the windward leg of the course).

Prepare yourself ahead of the race by getting an idea of what the characteristics are on the particular day. If you are sailing in your home waters, you will have a good idea of how the local weather operates, and what to expect. If you are sailing in a venue you do not know well, ask questions, get an idea of what to anticipate when certain characteristics occur.

Whatever the situation, the wind will never be entirely consistent in direction. A very good way to find out what is happening is to be out on the race course early. Sail to windward consistently and check your compass heading, or the wind direction, every five minutes or so. A pattern may well emerge. You could find, for instance, that the wind is oscillating over 10 degrees every 10 minutes. This will help you decide on which end of the starting line to begin; it will also enable you to work out when shifts are going to occur, which will help you plan your first beat.

Steady Change in Wind Direction

The wind may start blowing from a certain direction, and during the day swing slowly and steadily over, say, 90 degrees, before it stabilizes in the new direction. Measuring the wind direction before the start could indicate such a swing and your race could be planned accordingly. If there are meaningful swings, remember that the race officer can (and often does) move the windward mark.

Above *Looking for the leeward mark.*

The Laylines

The laylines (*see* illustration below) are the close-hauled courses (sailing as close to the wind as possible) to the windward mark, known as port or starboard laylines depending on which side of the course is being referred to.

Important note: the layline changes every time the wind switches. For this reason it is usually not a good plan to go out to the layline early. If you do and you encounter a lift, you could overstand (overshoot) the weather mark by several boat lengths – which have now been thrown away!

Leave your final tack for the layline until you are fairly close to the mark. Try to approach the mark on starboard tack (with right of way). A boat approaching the mark on port tack has virtually no rights and will normally meet a string of starboard tack boats which she will have to avoid, usually losing a lot of ground in the process.

Tacking on Headers

Headers are changes in wind direction which force a sailboat to pull off to adjust to the new direction. Wind lifts allow the boat to point up. Normally you would tack on headers – which, on the opposite tack, would be a lift. Tacking on every header will result in a shorter distance being sailed to the windward mark – which tends to indicate that headers are bad and lifts are good, but this is not always the case. If you are ahead and to leeward of a competitor, a lift could take that lead away. There is little you can do about it – if you tacked, you would be tacking into what would be a header on the other tack.

The Ladder Rung

A good way of understanding how wind switches affect sailboat racing is to imagine that each boat is towing the rung of a ladder, exactly at right angles to the wind, behind it. Every boat on that ladder rung, even if the distance between boats covers a mile, is equal. Remember that every wind switch alters the rung, and the positions of the sailboats on it.

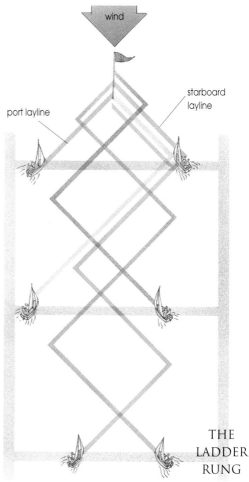

THE
LADDER
RUNG

Above *L26 One-Designs racing for the Lipton Challenge Cup in South Africa.*

Separation

If you decide that the starboard side of the course will pay and you head out towards that side after the start, and for various reasons a competitor decides that the port side will pay, the boats will soon be separated by a big distance, perhaps a mile or more. Now even a small shift in wind direction will make a very big difference in distance from the mark. Only let competitors get far away from you if you are sure your choice of strategy is correct.

If you are not certain which side of the course is going to pay, or some competitors go out on the starboard side while others go out on the port side, an option is to play the centre of the course. Still using the headers and lifts to the best of your ability, this is often safer than taking a long leg out to one or other side of the course.

CURRENTS AND TOPOGRAPHY

So far, only the wind has been considered, but a current, or an incoming or outgoing tide, can play a role in tactics too. Find out about normal current paths, check the tide tables and also consider how the local topography affects wind direction and strengths.

Left *Rounding the windward mark in close quarters.*

Following pages *The winning boat* Endeavour, *from New Zealand, competing for the Heineken Trophy in 1994 in the Whitbread Round-the-World Race.*

CHAPTER EIGHT

LONG-DISTANCE CRUISING

Top *Sextant, used in celestial navigation.*

For many who sail offshore boats, the ultimate objective is to set off on an ocean voyage, and for those who live in colder climates, the lure of the tropics is often irresistible. Many long-distance cruises are undertaken mainly in the trade-wind zones – the trades being those reliable winds to the north and south of the Equator which will take sailboats steadily westwards, across the Atlantic, Pacific and Indian oceans (although with today's modern yachts, it is not essential to follow these routes). North of the Equator the trades blow from a north-easterly direction, while in the southern hemisphere they blow from a southeasterly direction. It was the trade winds that enabled early navigators, with ships that did not go to windward well, to make their voyages of discovery.

WEATHER PATTERNS

Those who wish to make long ocean voyages will need to have some understanding of the world's weather systems. The northeast trades and southeast trades are separated by a band of light, variable winds, in the approximate vicinity of the equator, known as 'the doldrums'. They are often frustrating and difficult to sail through, particularly with heavy craft that are not fast in light weather. The trade winds stretch roughly from the doldrums to close to latitude 30 degrees north and 30 degrees south. North or south of the trades, depending on the hemisphere, is again an area of variable winds, beyond which you find the Westerlies of the northern and southern hemispheres.

A comfortable, modern cruising yacht.

Cyclones, Hurricanes and Typhoons

Cyclones, hurricanes and typhoons are tropical revolving storms which, as most people know, can sink vessels and wreak incredible damage when they reach the shore. The basic trade wind and westerly wind systems prevail all year round. The Westerlies tend to get stronger in winter, while specific sectors of the trade-wind routes are prone to cyclones, typhoons and hurricanes at certain times. These areas should be avoided during the season. Very briefly, between January and March, cyclones can develop in the Indian Ocean from Madagascar to Western Australia. During the same period, typhoons can develop in the western Pacific, reaching as far as the Australian east coast. The southeast trades become patchy in the western Pacific during

THE WORLD'S WEATHER SYSTEMS

January - March

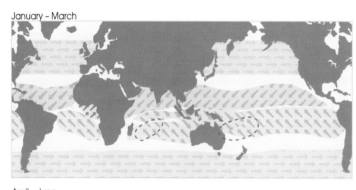

Typhoons
Tropical cyclones

Variable winds

SE Trade

NE Trade

Westerlies

Doldrums

Monsoon

April - June

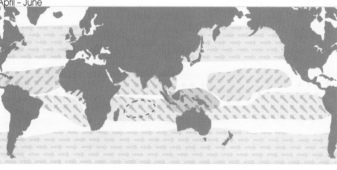

July - September

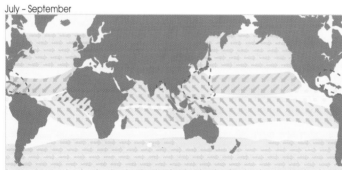

October - December

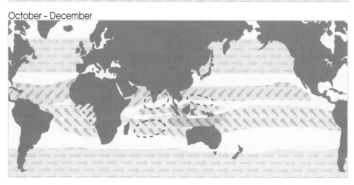

this period. From April to June, cyclones are still possible in the Indian Ocean, occurring from Madagascar to Western Australia.

July to September brings the hurricane season to the Caribbean area and the eastern seaboard of southern United States, while on the east coast of China, including a large area of the western Pacific, typhoons are possible. There is also a smallish area in the vicinity of northeast India, Bangladesh and northwest Burma where cyclones could occur.

October to December sees the possibility of cyclones in the Indian Ocean and in the north and south of India, with typhoons in the North Pacific and cyclones in the South Pacific.

With weather patterns being so clearly defined, there is a right and a wrong time to undertake ocean passages, which is well understood by sailors. Few tempt fate and sail their craft outside of the understood seasons. To help the sailor gauge weather patterns, the pilot charts issued by various authorities are invaluable. The US Navy and British Admiralty pilot charts are commonly used by sailors worldwide. For instance, the US charts are divided into five-degree rectangles. In the centre of the rectangle is a small blue circle in which the percentage of calms for the month is entered. The prevailing winds are shown by a series of arrows, the length indicating the proportion of wind expected from that direction, i.e. 35 means 35% of the wind from that month is expected from the direction shown. The arrows have tails, or feathers, and the number of feathers indicates the average force of the wind expressed by the Beaufort scale.

Gales (winds of above Force 8) are shown in red on a small inset chart. Currents are also shown on these charts, usually in green. The pilot charts are available for each ocean, by month. They will yield much of the information needed to get a good picture of the weather along the planned route.

Roaring Forties

The Roaring Forties occur in the Southern Ocean, where the winds blow exceptionally hard, and are not for the average sailor. This is the terrain of the Whitbread racers or the BT Challenge yachts. However, many conservative, safe voyages have been made by sailing to the north of the Forties, say about latitude 35 degrees south. At the right time of the year (that is, during the summer months) you can experience good winds here, mostly with a westerly component, without exposing yourself to the dangers of the Forties themselves. This route can be adopted for the passages between South America and South Africa, from South Africa to Australia and New Zealand, and from Australia and New Zealand to South America.

TROUBLE SPOTS

Unfortunately, even in today's modern world, there are plenty of trouble spots, which results in there being some definite 'no go' areas for pleasure yachts. Keep up to date with current affairs; yachting magazines and your country's sailing authorities should be able to advise on problem areas. Unbelievable as it may sound, modern pirates are active in certain regions, and these should be avoided by yachts; alternatively they should sail through the area accompanied by another boat. Incidents have occurred in the past in parts of South America, the Caribbean, the Red Sea, the Gulf of Suez and some areas of the Far East. However, the situation varies with changing economic and political circumstances, so one needs to be aware and to keep up to date.

ERIC AND SUSAN HISCOCK

For many years Eric and Susan Hiscock were the world's most famous cruising couple. Eric owned *Wanderer I*, then *Wanderer II*, which was designed and built for him just before World War II. They started cruising together in the 24ft (7m) *Wanderer II*, which they sailed from England to the Azores and back in 1950. The 30ft (9,1m) *Wanderer III*, designed by J Laurent Giles, was then built for them in England. They commenced their first circumnavigation in 1952, and at the same time Eric started producing the well-written and beautifully illustrated magazine articles and books that made the *Wanderers* and their owners so well known around the world.

The Hiscocks, through their writing and lecture tours, were responsible for helping many aspirant cruising sailors to take the plunge and actually do it. Their books, many of which are still in print, made excellent reading and were always most instructive. In addition, Eric was an excellent photographer, and his own photographs were used to illustrate the books.

After *Wanderer III*, which the Hiscocks owned for 16 years, came the large 49ft (15m) steel ketch *Wanderer IV*, built in the Netherlands. After serving them for 15 years, she was sold in New Zealand. The Hiscocks then had their last boat, *Wanderer V* (39ft; 12m), designed and built in New Zealand. Aboard her they made voyages to Australia as well as passages in the Pacific.

Eric Hiscock believed that cruising sailors should be self-sufficient, be prepared for any emergency and not expect outside help if trouble occurred. This theme was routinely highlighted in most of Hiscock's writing and still holds good for today's cruising sailors. The Hiscocks played a valuable role in encouraging amateur sailors to make competent and safe passages. At the time of writing, all the *Wanderers*, from *II* to *V*, were still in commission in various parts of the world.

PLANNING THE VOYAGE

Give some thought to the sights you are anticipating seeing and the lifestyle you want to lead. Note that many small vessels make long voyages these days, particularly along the trade wind routes, and some popular ports of call are positively overcrowded in season. No longer is it a novelty for a foreign yacht to enter port, and it is now more difficult than it was 30 or 40 years ago – when voyaging in small yachts was in its infancy – to get to know the locals.

In the colder, higher latitudes in both hemispheres, cruising yachts are rarer and the way you are received can be somewhat warmer. Crowded anchorages are mostly a rarity.

Left *A fold-up bike, like this one on the* Claude Neon, *allows crew members to explore when they berth in new destinations.*

Above Drumbeat, *a US-designed but British-built wooden racer cruiser.*

Bottom *A Bowman 42, a fairly heavy displacement blue water (deep-sea) cruiser.*

THE VESSEL

Many different types of sailing craft have made successful long voyages. The choice of craft is really open and depends on how much money is available, whether you are prepared to live in a somewhat 'minimalist' way, or whether you want as many home comforts as possible.

Some 20-footers have made seamanlike passages around the world – but while they can be extremely seaworthy, by their very size their accommodation- and weight-carrying ability is limited. English-born John Guzzwell, who made his name in the late 1950s by sailing his home-built 21ft (6,4m) *Trekka* round the world, starting and ending in Vancouver, said that her small size never bothered him at sea. However, in port she was so small that he could not entertain or invite visitors down below.

As your requirements increase, more electrical power is required, and more extra weight must be carried. Weight destroys a boat's performance, so a happy medium must be achieved. The more you want in a boat, the bigger that boat will have to be.

If you have chosen a monohull, make sure it is of a type suitable for long voyages and is self-righting. This can always be checked with the builders, or better still, the designers. Multihulls are also capable of making long passages, but they need to be designed for it. The hi-tech, high-speed multihulls used for record-breaking passages and short-handed races are very 'twitchy' to sail, can capsize easily, do not have much room inside, and should not be considered for cruising.

No one type of craft can be considered superior to another: full-keel craft; fin-keeled, shallow-hulled boats; double-enders; transom-sterned; high free-board and low freeboard; heavy and light boats – these have all made successful passages. The same applies to rigs. All types of rig have been used for voyaging. Today, with advanced self-steering to cope with higher-speed sailing, the sloop or cutter is the common choice.

Construction Methods and Maintenance

Maintenance must be considered very carefully when buying a boat for a long passage. Wood is a great building material, but traditionally built wooden boats tend to be old and they require a lot of maintenance even when they are new. This takes a lot of time and can be very expensive and difficult to carry out in foreign ports.

The majority of world cruisers these days are fibreglass with aluminium spars. This is probably one of the best combinations for a good-looking, reliable boat that needs a minimum of maintenance. Steel is

also a very good and strong building material, but even if well prepared and coated at the outset, maintenance will inevitably be higher than with fibreglass boats. However, with the very real dangers these days of hitting partially submerged containers and whales – or rocks/coral reefs – a steel structure could well be best when it comes to impact resistance.

Aluminium is also a good building material and, if the correct grade of aluminium is used, the result is an excellent boat. Electrolysis can be a problem with aluminium, and must be guarded against by first applying a good coating on the aluminium, and by using a system of anodes (*see* box).

Modern wood construction is excellent, too. Strip-planked and cold-moulded wooden hulls can be immensely strong and have a long life, particularly if covered with a layer of fibreglass saturated with epoxy resin. Epoxy resin is far more expensive than the polyester resins used for normal fibreglass construction, but it is much more impervious to water absorption. It would be wise to have the bottom of a stock fibreglass hull stripped of its paint and its outer layer of gel coat, then to have an epoxy or an epoxy fibreglass layer applied. This would definitely help prevent osmosis (the absorption of water) and the resultant small bubbles, which does affect some stock fibreglass hulls.

Collisions have been touched on. The question is: is there anything that can be done to lessen damage, or the chance of sinking? There is, but it will take away some storage space – a small price to pay for minimizing the chance of sinking. The forward section of the bow can definitely be strengthened, but even more important is to create a watertight compartment in the boat's forward section. Many cruising sailboats have a V-berth in the forward cabin, which can usually be converted into a watertight compartment. It can also be filled with foam, but this would entail having to sacrifice some storage space. While this exercise is only effective if the hull in the forward section is damaged, this is where most collision damage occurs. Whatever the construction method, bear the maintenance issue in mind. You do not want to spend too much of your time in port having to maintain your boat.

Ship's Papers

Laws differ from country to country, but many maritime nations allow you to register small craft as 'ships' and thereby obtain a set of ship's papers. These are extremely useful to have: they confirm ownership, establish the country from which the yacht originates, and can be of use if you encounter trouble in foreign ports. They are invaluable if you need the help of your country's consulate, or if you wish to sell your craft in a foreign port.

Whether you register as a ship or not, buy a waterproof file for all the information pertaining to your yacht: official registration, registration with your club or national body, your ship's radio station licence, life-raft service certificate, local permission (from your home port) to operate at sea, and your own personal nautical qualifications. Together with the clearance papers from your last port of call, such a file is usually accepted as ship's papers. When you leave a country at an official port of entry or exit, you will probably have to clear with:

Port Health

Customs

Immigration (passport control)

Port Authority.

Remember to check if you need visas for visiting certain countries. Check also on health requirements such as inoculation for yellow fever and the like.

ANODES

Anodes are sacrificial plates or cylindrical-shaped pieces of zinc fitted to the hull of a boat. When electrolytical action occurs, they corrode, or waste away, thus saving the hull itself – as well as propellors, propellor and rudder shafts, and skin fittings – from electrolytic decay. They are replaced from time to time.

Below and right *A typical galley as featured on board Alpha 50. A modern boat of this size is likely to carry a top-opening fridge.*

Right, bottom *A barbecue cooker facility fixed to the stern of the boat.*

FOOD AND WATER

Food

Canned foods play an important role here. As the labels could soak off and clog the pumps, it is best to remove these and record the contents on the can. Plenty of very palatable dehydrated and freeze-dried meals are available, but make sure you allow for the additional fresh water that will have to be added to these meals.

Fruit, such as apples and oranges, keeps well and can last for several weeks on board. For vegetables, onions and potatoes are long-lasting (onions really do perk up a meal). Eggs covered with Vaseline have a life of many months, as does bacon left in its supermarket packaging, especially if packed on top of water tanks, which helps to keep it cool. This also applies to cheese. Thus, your basic canned, dehydrated, or freeze-dried food can be supplemented by some fresh food every day. Of course, the choice is much wider if you have refrigeration. However, marine refrigerators can sometimes go wrong and back-up emergency stores should be carried on board.

Tupperware, or similar sealable plastic containers, are very useful for keeping sugar, biscuits, flour (for the baking of bread at sea – excellent recipes exist), etc., fresh and dry. They are invaluable for the modern sailor, as they can also be used for storing dry cell batteries, spares, tools, flares, and other items.

It is wise to have your proposed diet checked out by a doctor or dietician before you go, to ensure you have achieved the correct balance. He or she could well prescribe some multivitamin tablets to ensure continuous good health.

Water

All seagoing sailboats have some water tankage, but not always enough for a long voyage – additional tankage will have to be installed. Stainless steel is good but expensive, and steel tanks will probably have to be professionally made. In fibreglass vessels, tanks can be built in. The basic tank can be made up in plywood and covered with fibreglass; epoxy is the better resin for this purpose. The tanks will need baffles to subdue the surging effect of the water.

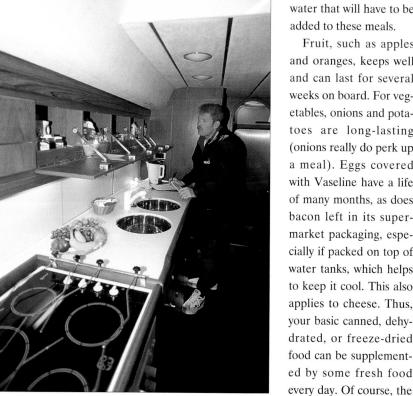

There are many water makers (for desalinating sea water) on the market these days, and they can certainly be considered to supply a large percentage of your water requirements, provided you have adequate electrical power. Ensure that you always have fresh water backup. At worst, a person can exist for some time on two litres of water per day, even in the tropics.

Water in some ports is not to be trusted and it will do no harm to carry a water-purifying additive.

FIRST-AID KIT

For long voyages, a well-stocked medical box is essential. A good method is to divide this into two sections: one for first aid, the second for more serious medicines. The first-aid container would carry such items as sticking plaster, disinfectant, headache pills or powders, bandages, safety pins, antiseptic cream, burn cream, and laxatives. The medical box itself should carry antibiotics, strong painkillers, and a variety of drugs suggested by your doctor, together with sterile sutures to stitch wounds. A list of all medications should be glued inside the container, together with brief instructions for their use. Major medical problems have not been that common at sea in small craft, but you must consider the possibilities. Coral cuts are difficult to heal and must be treated. Burns from cooking are one of the most common injuries and you should be prepared to treat these. Broken ribs also occur, but at sea, all that can be done is to keep the patient as still as possible. Splints should be carried to immobilize broken limbs until assistance can be obtained. Illnesses such as appendicitis have also occurred at sea, but the right drugs can usually keep this at bay until port is reached.

Several excellent books are available on medical problems on small craft at sea and at least one of these should be carried on board. In addition one or two crew members should take a first-aid course and be proficient in artificial respiration, stitching of wounds and other basic first-aid tasks.

In serious cases, help can be obtained via long-range radio, or communication by satellite if the sailboat carries this equipment. It is good practice for the crew to have a general medical and dental examination before setting out on a cruise.

BASIC CONTENTS OF A FIRST-AID BOX

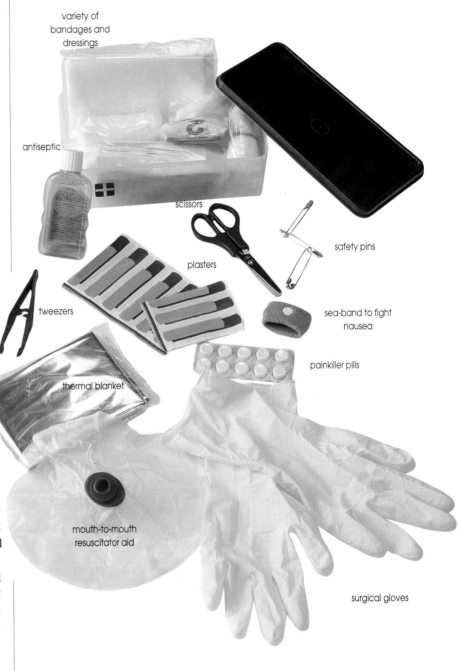

variety of bandages and dressings

antiseptic

scissors

safety pins

plasters

tweezers

sea-band to fight nausea

painkiller pills

thermal blanket

mouth-to-mouth resuscitator aid

surgical gloves

Right *Wind vane self-steering gear.*

Right *Radio, radar, GPS, wind generator and life raft.*

SELF-STEERING

Twin Headsails

Even if you are a keen sailor and helmsman, steering a cruising boat 24 hours a day on a long passage will soon become very tedious! Self-steering of some sort is essential.

In the earlier days of voyaging, between the two world wars and following World War II, boats could be made to steer downwind by booming out two headsails, one to port and one to starboard. The sheets of each were led to the tiller. If the boat headed up, the pressure on the sheet of the windward headsail increased. This pulled the tiller to windward and put the boat back on course. While effective, this method had several drawbacks:

- Twin headsails could only be used downwind, with a course variation of about 20 degrees each way
- Rhythmic rolling tended to set in during trade-wind passages
- Not that much sail area was carried, so the rig was not particularly fast.

Wind Vane Gear

A breakthrough came with vane steering, developed from model yachts. Driven by the force of the wind, the vane can transfer its power to the steering system in several ways. It can act directly on a trim-tab hinged to transom-hung rudders, it can be indirectly connected to wheels or tillers, or it can drive independent rudders to supplement main rudders. The power produced by the vane can also be increased by the use of servo pendulums (similar to long thin rudders but pivoted horizontally at the top); as the blade is turned by the wind vane, it tends to kick up with a force that's transferred by lines to the wheel or tiller.

Research will indicate what vane system is suitable for your boat. The beauty of it is that it's driven by the wind, so it does not need electrical power. The advantages of a vane system over the twin headsail system are:

- It can be used on all points of sail
- Fore-and-aft rig can be used
- Faster passage speeds are possible.

Autopilots

Often, developments in racing filter down to cruising boats. One of these is the electronic autopilot. The single-handed racers used vanes for many years but, inevitably, as the boats developed and multi-hulls came on the scene, they became much faster. Eventually the point was reached where vane gear could not handle the speeds being achieved and small autopilots began to be developed in earnest.

At first they were unreliable, consumed a lot of electrical power, and single-handed racers had to take several spares along for a race. Nowadays the gear is compact, reliable and strong enough to do the job. In addition, it can be interfaced with electronic compasses, GPS's, and really does warrant the name 'autopilot'. However, it uses electricity, which has to be generated on a regular basis.

ELECTRICAL POWER

No matter how few electronic devices you decide to have, rare is the ocean-going sailboat today that can exist without electricity. This presents two main problems: how to generate it and how to store it.

Most auxiliary sailboats have a diesel engine these days, and the alternator integral with the engine can be a major source of power generation. It might seem like overkill, but if you are to rely on the main engine for power generation, then a spare alternator and a spare starter motor should be carried. Alternators are not items that the average man can repair at sea. Over the past 15 years or so, the trend with marine diesels for the leisure market has been to make them lighter. This is a really worthwhile development, but it has its bad points too. One is the difficulty of hand-starting these lightweight diesels as they have no flywheel, in contrast to the previous generation of diesels where the engine could be spun by hand with the decompression levers lifted. The inertia of the flywheel would keep the engine turning while the decompression levers were dropped, starting the engine. However, there is little inertia generated in the modern engine, and when it is cranked by hand, it tends to stop dead as soon as the decompression levers are dropped. Battery power and a working starter motor are therefore essential.

Many other devices can be used to generate at least a portion of the boat's power requirements. A good example is the solar panel. These have improved tremendously in recent times, and can generate a worthwhile amount of additional electrical current. However, they will only keep working provided there is enough sunlight (although modern panels

do work in overcast conditions) and, if the boat is left for any length of time, they could overcharge the batteries, thereby damaging them. Solar panels should therefore be connected through a voltage regulator, in much the same way as an alternator is.

Wind generators are also popular, and operate effectively in quite light winds. However, in strong winds they revolve at high speeds and could injure anyone coming into contact with the blades. They are also very noisy. Working out a way to stop the blades revolving in strong winds is advisable. Again,

Above and below *Boats carrying solar panels.*

wind generators should be connected via a voltage regulator to prevent the batteries from overcharging.

Water generators, where the propellers are turned by the boat's movement through the water, are also a possibility. However, unlike wind generators and solar panels, they will only work when the boat is under way.

Small petrol generators are useful for charging and an added advantage is that they can be used for operating AC devices, such as electric tools. However, unless specially mounted, they can only be used in reasonable weather. In addition, petrol (gasoline) needs to be carried on board, although a sailboat can carry some petrol for the dinghy's outboard motor. Bear in mind that petrol is highly flammable and should be treated accordingly.

Larger sailboats are able to accommodate separate small diesel-charging plants, which is an efficient method of supplying power.

Batteries

Batteries are the usual method of storing power in sailboats. A lead acid battery, similar to those used in motor vehicles, can be used. These have not been designed for deep-cycle operation and they deteriorate fairly quickly during marine use; perhaps two years can be considered an average lifetime for them. A better choice would be the deep-cycle batteries developed for marine and caravan use.

In addition there are now on the market a number of sealed batteries, working on various principles. These need no maintenance, are normally deep-cycle batteries and have a longer life than the standard lead acid type of battery.

The smallest ocean-crossing sailboat probably has two batteries. These should be installed as two separate banks, i.e. power will be drawn from one battery at a time. This avoids the possibility of running both batteries flat simultaneously. In large boats, more batteries should be carried, but they need to be installed in two or more banks, activated by a master switch. A dedicated engine-starting battery is recommended if it can be accommodated. Always put

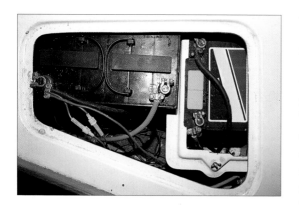

Below A yacht's batteries neatly stored.
Right bottom and opposite top *Different arrangements for storing life rafts on a boat, although the stowage of the soft valise is extremely exposed and is not an ideal position.*

isolator switches on the positive and negative sides of the battery circuits, and isolate the batteries when the boat is left, even for a short period of time.

LIFE RAFTS

Most ocean-crossing sailboats carry self-inflating life rafts – in fact some countries insist they are carried for passage making. When purchasing a life raft, bear in mind that they are made to different standards for different applications. Some are meant for coastal use, some for deep-sea use and some for semi-Arctic conditions where tests have proved normal rafts fail to inflate fully. Buy the raft most suitable for the passages you have in mind.

Most small-craft rafts come with the option of fibreglass or soft valises. The hard valise is obviously more durable, particularly if the raft is to be stowed on deck. If the raft is going to be stowed in a dry compartment, a soft valise can be an option.

When craft are laid up for winter, store the raft ashore in a dry area. This serves to increase the useful life of the raft considerably. In addition, the raft within its valise should not be sat on, stepped on or generally abused; rough treatment could open the joints of a hard valise sufficiently to admit water. Unless this is detected immediately and the raft taken to a service station right away, it could be irreparably damaged.

Make sure that your life-raft stowage not only prevents damage to the raft, but allows the raft to be thrown overboard in the minimum amount of time. Make sure that the raft's painter is securely fastened inside the parent vessel.

The minimum should be a Very High Frequency (VHF) transceiver (a combination of transmitter and receiver), essential for talking to the authorities in the various ports being visited; and an all-wave receiving set, preferably one which also has the facility to receive Single Side Band (SSB) as well as normal AM signals.

VHF radio operates on the principle of what is termed 'line of sight', meaning that the maximum range is only about 30 nautical miles (except when freak atmospheric conditions occur), possibly the distance between a small craft and a shore station. As shore stations place their antennae at the highest possible point, the range between them and small craft is the longest possible. The range between craft at sea is therefore not nearly as great. Sailboats can maximize the range of their VHF by placing the antenna at the top of the mast.

Different life rafts have different contents, and most need to be supplemented with a 'grabbag'. It should be waterproof, or consist of a number of waterproof canisters, which will float.

Familiarize yourself with the contents of the raft and then carefully consider what to put into the grab-bag (which must be easily accessible in an emergency): additional food, medical supplies, torches, fishing gear, knives, additional distress flares, and passport, credit cards and money. A hand-held VHF radio (see below), preferably a waterproof one, and a hand-held GPS are a good idea. Water is vital. Some 2gal (10-litre) plastic jerry cans, slightly underfilled (leaving an air space so that they will float), should be prepared in case the raft has to be used.

Rafts need to be serviced regularly to have a valid certificate. A good recommendation is to be at the service station when the raft is opened and inflated, to familiarize yourself with how big (or small) it is, exactly what it contains and how it works.

Only take to the life raft as an absolute last resort. A number of abandoned sailboats have been found afloat months after their crews left them, believing they were in immediate danger of sinking.

COMMUNICATIONS
VHF Transceivers and All-wave Receivers
The sort of communication equipment needed to embark on a voyage depends on exactly what your objectives are and how much money is available.

VHF is comparatively inexpensive, and it is worthwhile carrying a hand-held set as a backup. Many of these are waterproof, which makes them ideal for use in an emergency. Most are self-contained, being powered by penlight or rechargeable batteries, and most can be connected to the 12-volt main ship's power supply. An inexpensive safety measure is a portable antenna, which stows in a very small space and which can simply plug in to the main ship's set in the case of a dismasting. All-wave receivers, particularly those able to receive on SSB

Above *An amateur radio set, known as 'ham' radio.*

Above *Satellite antennae and radar scanner.*

SSB is not nearly as simple as VHF to operate, and the frequencies used have to be varied according to distance and time of the day. A licence to use SSB is therefore more complicated and somewhat more difficult to obtain than that for VHF.

Ham sets, intended to be operated by amateurs with some knowledge of radios, are more complex and not as foolproof as marine sets. They are also not as resistant to a marine atmosphere, but they do allow communication with radio amateurs all over the world. 'Maritime radio nets' are run by amateurs worldwide. They have regular daily schedules ('skeds') with ocean sailors, who are encouraged to report in each day, and offer weather information and local advice, very useful to the ocean voyager approaching a country with which he is not familiar. To become a licensed ham, examinations which are fairly consistent around the world must be taken. The Amateur Radio League or similar organization will give you the requirements for your country.

Most marine sets can be adapted easily to operate on the ham bands, and vice versa. If the sailor possesses both licences, the authorities in some countries will allow one transceiver to be licensed for both marine and ham bands.

The two transceivers can use the sailboat's backstay, or a whip antenna. To operate well, installation is very important. The transceiver has to be earthed, either to the keel or a special earthing plate, and the lead to the backstay or whip antenna should be as short as possible. An antenna tuner (sometimes built into the set) is required to tune the set to the antenna for operation on different frequencies. Both SSB transceivers can provide good service once their limitations have been understood.

Communication via Satellite

Satellite communications are presently expensive. However, most of the large 'superyachts' carry this type of equipment, as do the Whitbread Round-the-World racers and the BT Challenge yachts. Systems such as Inmarsat C and others enable communication by voice, fax and e-mail. This equipment is not normally carried by the thousands of cruising yachts making passages on the oceans of the world. There is much talk about cellular phones being developed which will operate via satellite; they could well make the above equipment obsolete. The first of these is expected to be on the market in the year 2000.

as well, enable you to receive a wide variety of broadcasts including commercial stations, marine coast stations, weather reports and accurate time signals – essential for navigation by sextant.

Long-range Communication

The most cost-effective method of long-distance communication is SSB radio. Satellite communication is the ultimate, but it is expensive. The average sailor would choose SSB first.

Two types of SSB transceivers are often found on ocean-crossing sailboats: marine sets and ham (amateur radio) sets. Both types have to be licensed. Your first choice should be a marine set. This enables the operator to work the coast stations around the world, and make ship-to-shore telephone calls. Weekly or more frequent schedules can be set up in advance to make such contacts easier. Marine SSB also enables ship-to-ship communication over considerable distances.

NAVIGATION

Accurate navigation at sea was once one of the prospective ocean voyager's biggest concerns. Now, thanks to the GPS (*see* page 93), this is no longer so. Until the mid-1980s, the primary manner in which the small-craft navigator found his way across the oceans was celestial navigation: determining the angle of the sun and, for the more knowledgeable, the moon, planets and stars, with a sextant. Exact Universal Time (formerly Greenwich Mean Time) together with the angle measured, the current year's nautical almanac and a book of tables, made it possible to work out a position line. For sailors wanting to do simple celestial navigation, it was necessary only to obtain a position line from the sun in the morning, and, coupled with a noon sight (latitude at noon), they could fix their position once a day. This was sufficient to navigate safely, provided one's DR was meticulously kept up between fixes. Caution had to be exercised when approaching land which was not easily visible, such as low-lying coral atolls.

The first major breakthrough in several centuries came with the release of the US Satnav system for general use in about 1985. This system used the Transit Satellites and allowed a good fix (an accurate calculation of one's position) perhaps 10 to 15 times in a 24-hour period, depending on satellite positioning. It was a major advance on celestial navigation. Not many years later, in about 1990, the GPS system became operational. Today, some very good GPS hand-held units are sold at less than the cost of a hand-held VHF transceiver.

For passage-making today, a fitted GPS, plus at least one hand-held GPS, is sufficient. If you have the misfortune to experience a major power failure, it will knock out the main GPS. Here, the hand-held backup comes into play. It works on penlight batteries, although battery consumption is unfortunately high. To make the most economical use of a hand-held system, switch it on only when you want to fix your position, switching it off again immediately. An advantage is that it can be taken in a life raft if the yacht has to be abandoned.

While the basic function of a GPS is to fix one's position accurately, it provides many other functions. It gives speed, altitude above or below sea level, direction of travel, time and routes. Waypoints (the points a sailor wants to reach) can also be programmed in.

In spite of the convenience and accuracy of GPS, it is still a good idea to have a sextant, nautical almanac and tables on board. A basic knowledge of how to take and work out sun sights does ensure added peace of mind.

Charts

The traditional paper chart is beginning to be replaced by electronic charts (*see* page 95), compatible with the many different navigation systems that come with a display screen. These systems are installed on larger yachts, and require electrical power as well as costing a fair amount of money. Paper charts will have a major role to play for many years to come. Unfortunately, they have become very expensive, and are bulky to carry for a long voyage. However, yachtsmen the world over are prepared to swap charts, trading those of areas they have visited for those of areas they intend visiting.

It is wise to have a chart for each ocean you cross. Each day, at specific times, the craft's position should be marked, making a permanent record of the passage. This position, the day's run, and other relevant information should then be entered in the boat's log book.

CHAPTER NINE

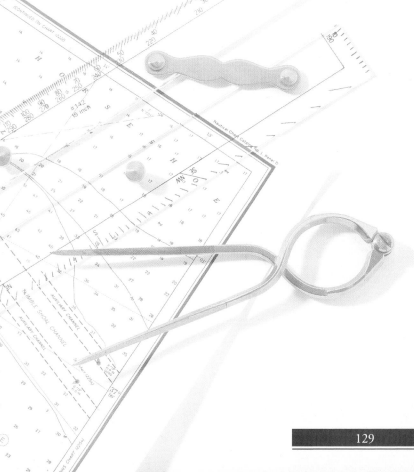

SEAMANSHIP AND SAFETY

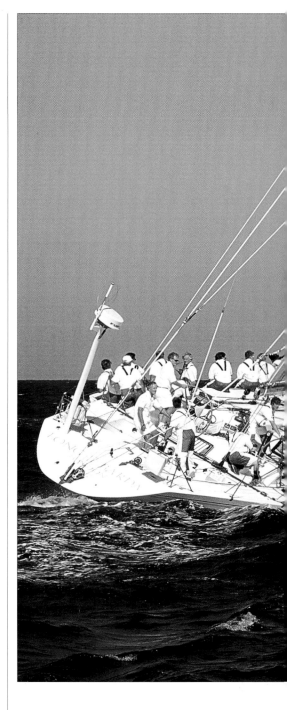

Seamanship is essential for remaining safe in open water and at sea. Even top-level round-the-buoy sailors need a degree of seamanship, such as the ability to tie basic knots or to gauge the weather. The age in which we live is one where we are in some ways looked after too well: if one's car breaks down, one calls the Automobile Association on the cell phone. This has tended to flow through to boating, where more and more of the rescue authorities' call-outs involve towing in craft, many of which could have got back to port themselves (and, 20 years ago, almost certainly would have). It is so easy to use the VHF radio and ask for help when conditions are bad and one is wet, cold and hungry, but not really in danger. This is a trend which should be resisted; the rescue services should only be called out in really serious circumstances. The more you know about seamanship, safety and health, the less likely you are to have to call for help.

ROPES AND KNOTS
Basic knowledge of ropes, rope work and knots is an essential part of being a good seaman. The fibres discussed in Types of Sailcloth (*see* pages 58–59)

have also played an important role in rope development. First, the synthetic fibres nylon and Dacron, then Kevlar, Spectra and Vectran, were added to rope, increasing their strength and creating a low-stretch product. As a result, modern ropes last longer and, unlike their natural-fibre predecessors, don't rot when left wet; they do, however, deteriorate from exposure to sunlight. Traditionally laid, three-strand

Halyards neatly coiled aboard a Dufour 35.

Boats taking part in the Middle Sea Race off Malta.

polyester ropes are excellent, long lasting, and are used extensively aboard cruisers and cruiser-racers. Like three-strand nylon ropes (which unlike polyester are stretchy and therefore most useful as anchor rodes and mooring lines), three-strand polyester ropes can be spliced, whipped and knotted in the traditional manner (*see* illustrations on page 132–135). Special nonstretch ropes containing Kevlar and other added fibres are more expensive, and tend to be used on hi-tech racing craft. A great many plaited ropes are available, varying from 8- to 16-plait, some with three-strand cores. These can be eye spliced and also spliced to flexible wire for use as halyards (ropes used for raising or lowering sails or yards), but splicing this type of rope is best left to the professional rigger. Many cruising yachts today

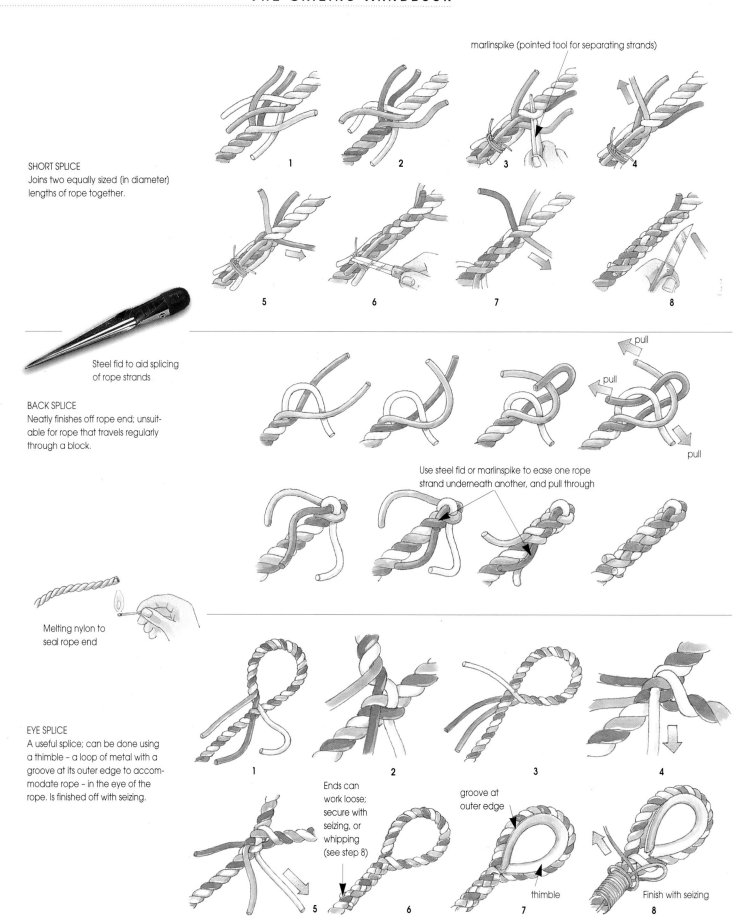

marlinspike (pointed tool for separating strands)

SHORT SPLICE
Joins two equally sized (in diameter) lengths of rope together.

1 2 3 4

5 6 7 8

Steel fid to aid splicing of rope strands

BACK SPLICE
Neatly finishes off rope end; unsuitable for rope that travels regularly through a block.

pull

pull

pull

Use steel fid or marlinspike to ease one rope strand underneath another, and pull through

Melting nylon to seal rope end

EYE SPLICE
A useful splice; can be done using a thimble – a loop of metal with a groove at its outer edge to accommodate rope – in the eye of the rope. Is finished off with seizing.

1 2 3 4

Ends can work loose; secure with seizing, or whipping (see step 8)

groove at outer edge

5 6 7 thimble 8 Finish with seizing

have reverted to all-rope halyards, omitting the wire section used by ocean-racing yachts to eliminate stretch, and relying on the low stretch of the pre-stretched polyester ropes.

Splicing three-strand rope is a very useful skill to acquire. A hollow stainless steel fid (used to pry open the strands) makes splicing heavy line easier. Traditional whipping (to bind with spirally wound twine) should be used to finish the ends of three-strand or plaited synthetic rope, after the ends have been heat-cut or sealed by burning. The step-by-step illustrations left, below, and on pages 134–135 show how to accomplish all the above procedures.

Various finishes and 'feels' can be achieved with synthetic fibres; for instance, ropes produced specially for sheets can be made fairly soft and therefore easier on the hands. Plaid or plaited ropes are also an option.

In spite of the development of synthetic-fibre ropes, the basic knots which have been in use for centuries have not changed. A sailor should be adept at tying the most useful of these without having to think about it.

Probably the most useful knot of all is the **bowline** (*see* page 134). It is the knot usually used to attach sheets to a sail, and it is suitable for many other applications. The bowline does not slip under load, but once the load is reduced or removed, it can easily be undone. The sailor should be able to tie this knot in any situation, under any conditions.

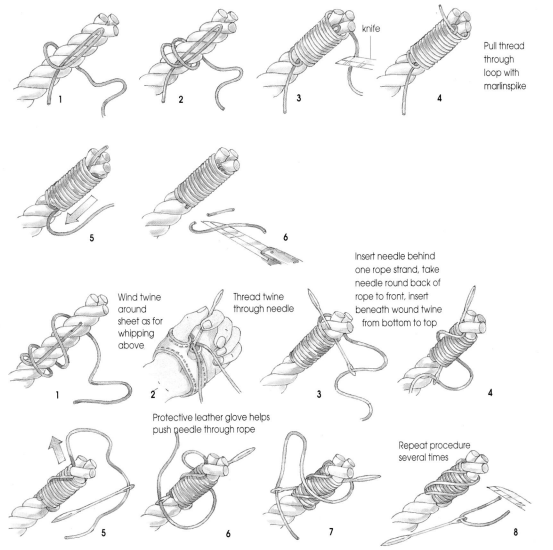

WHIPPING
Twine wound around the end of a sheet or halyard neatens the finish. Used in addition to heat-sealing where rope is synthetic.

PALM AND NEEDLE WHIPPING

The **reef knot**, also known as a square knot (*see* below), was, as its name implies, originally used for tying-in reefs in big sails (tying the reefing cringles when the sail is reefed or reduced in size). It is still used for this purpose, and also for joining two lengths of equal-diameter rope. The reef knot can be undone under load.

A **round turn and two half-hitches**, and a **clove hitch**, can be used to attach a line to a spar or mooring post. The **figure-of-eight knot**, very easy to tie, is used at the end of sheets to stop them slipping through blocks and leads.

A very important knot is the **rolling hitch** – it is essential in an emergency, such as when a big override causes a sheet to be jammed on a winch. A rope is attached to the jammed sheet, between the sail and the winch, using a rolling hitch. The tail of the rope is then taken to another winch, and winched in, thereby releasing the strain on the jammed sheet, and allowing it to be easily cleared. It is wise to practise these and other essential knots.

The correct methods of creating **sheet** and **double sheet bend** knots – used for tying ropes of different diameters together – and how to belay a rope around a cleat are also illustrated opposite.

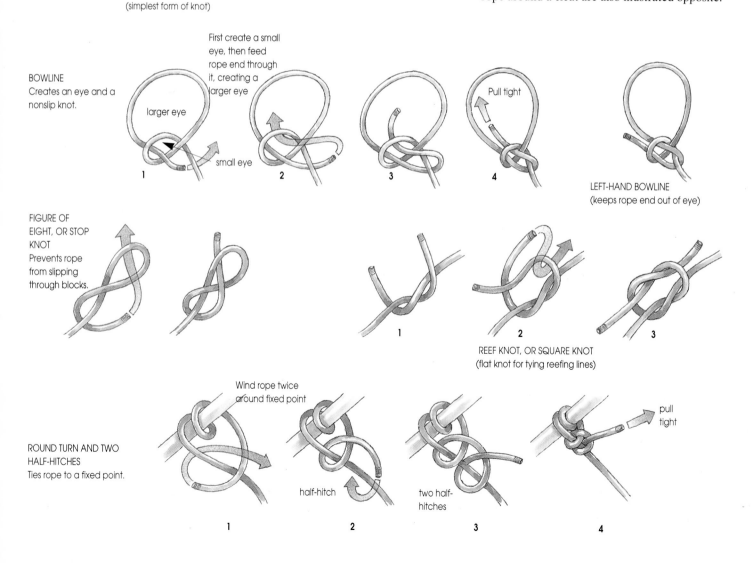

CLOVE HITCH
Hitch for tying rope
to spar or post.

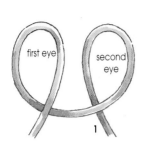

first eye

second eye

1

Line up first eye
with second eye

2

Slip both loops
over post

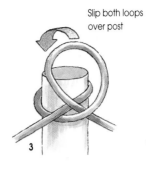

3

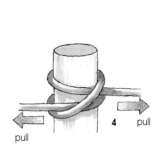

4 pull

pull

ROLLING HITCH
Ties a thin rope to
a thicker one.

Loop (or roll) thinner
rope twice around
thicker piece

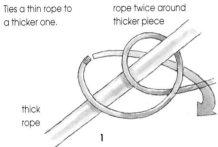

thick
rope

1

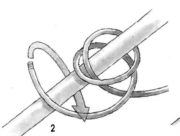

2

Form a
hitch

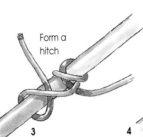

3

pull

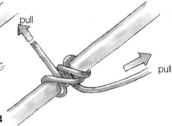

4

pull

SHEET BEND
Ties ropes of different
thicknesses together.

1

thinner rope

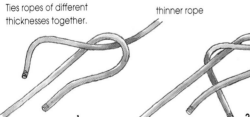

2

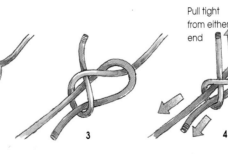

3

Pull tight
from either
end

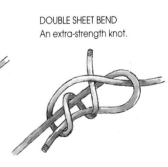

4

DOUBLE SHEET BEND
An extra-strength knot.

After winding rope for a full turn
round horn of cleat, form figure
of eight; repeat several times

BELAYING CLEAT

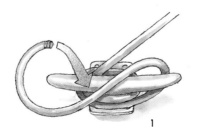

1

2

Opposite *Preparing to drop anchor.*

ANCHORS AND ANCHORING

The holding power of an anchor can be improved by using the correct ground tackle. Except on very small craft, the anchor should have a length of chain – the longer the better – between the anchor and the commencement of the anchor warp (also line, cable or rode).

To really feel secure when anchored, some cruising yachts use 100 per cent chain as an anchor rode. The amount of scope, or length of the anchor line, plays a major role in safe anchoring. As a rule of thumb, the scope should be at least five times the depth of the water.

Fisherman Anchor (Admiralty Anchor)

This is the traditionally shaped anchor. It is relatively inexpensive and stows flat. However, the stock (or cross arm) needs to be unfolded before it is lowered. Only in special circumstances, such as the presence of weed, is its holding power better than that of the plough (CQR), Danforth and Bruce anchors (described below).

Plough (CQR) Anchor

These anchors have a large fluke area and are popular among cruising sailors in spite of being cumbersome and somewhat difficult to stow.

Most ploughs have a strong hinge between the ploughshares and the shank, which assists the anchor to dig in. These are good all-round anchors, especially in sand and mud, and they dig in well in softer bottom soils.

Danforth Anchor

The Danforth anchor has big flukes which pivot about the shank, and it holds well, particularly in soft ground such as sand and mud. It stows flat – an important factor. The Danforth is a popular anchor on cruisers and cruiser-racers.

Bruce Anchor

The Bruce anchor is a one-piece casting, easily recognizable from its two curved horns which help the main fluke bury itself in the ground. It is a popular anchor which holds well.

Grapnel

This is a small four-fluked folding anchor. As it is not highly effective, it is best used by dinghies and small craft. Sometimes it is placed ashore and buried by hand. It plays a useful role for particularly small craft.

Plough (CQR) Anchor

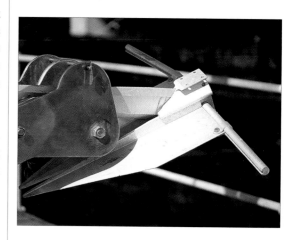

Danforth Anchor

Bruce Anchor

Choice of Anchors

A cruiser or offshore racer would probably carry two anchors: a plough or Bruce as the main anchor, while a typical choice for the second anchor is a Danforth. The main anchor has about 40ft (12m) of chain, the second anchor somewhat less. The anchor warps are in the vicinity of 150ft (45m) long. In order to save weight, the racer generally does not have an anchor windlass (a drum driven by a crank to aid raising the anchor), relying on crew power.

A serious cruising yacht is most likely to have three or more anchors, with two of these having an all-chain cable. The main anchor is permanently mounted, probably at the stem (or bow), ready to be released in an instant. A cruising craft of over 35ft (10.5m) almost certainly has an anchor windlass to ease the load of raising the anchor. Depending on the size of the boat, the windlass can be operated by hand or be electrically driven.

Cruising yachts also tend to carry far longer anchor chains than cruiser racers, as in some areas anchoring is a major factor of cruising. The yacht may have to anchor in bad weather or in some inhospitable spots, and skipper and crew must have confidence that the anchor, or anchors, will hold.

Anchoring Procedure

For serious anchoring, a good bow fitting with a roller (or rollers) and carefully shaped leads to avoid chafe, are absolutely necessary. For those who only anchor occasionally, such elaborate fittings are not necessary. However, chafe is an enemy and if you are anchoring with rope, the section of the rope that passes over the anchor roller, or through a fairlead, may have to be protected from chafe by lashing old rags around it, or using a split plastic tube.

When anchoring, know your position and check your chart. How deep is it? What sort of bottom is there? Are there any hazards, wrecks, underwater cables and the like? Confirm the depth with a depth finder if possible.

Be prepared to anchor with an anchor chain, or chain and warp combination, that's at least five times the depth of the water. In severe conditions, such as choppy water, fast-running tides and high winds, be prepared to increase the length of the warp, particularly if there is plenty of room to swing. The change in direction of the tide and wind must be anticipated when allowing for swinging room.

If the boat is under power, approach the anchoring spot heading upwind or, if the tide is predominant, against the tide. Make sure you have enough room to drop back as the anchor warp is paid out. Bring the boat to a standstill, drop the anchor and let the boat drop back, paying out the warp until the desired length has been reached (the warp should become taut, with the anchor digging in). A touch astern on the engine should help bed in the anchor.

Anchoring under sail would be similar, except the boat would be luffed head to wind to stop her, good judgement being necessary to ensure she stops in the area in which the anchor is to be dropped. Once the anchor is on the bottom and has bitten in, sails can be lowered. Find some landmarks on which to take bearings and ensure the boat is not moving (that is, dragging her anchor).

Sometimes, anchors snag something on the bottom, and can be very difficult to raise. Here a tripping line can be of great help. Most anchors have a hole near their base, through which a tripping line can be tied, or shackled. This line is then buoyed or, to prevent it being cut by a passing power boat, brought back to the boat. When the time comes to raise the anchor, if all is well, the tripping line is recovered as the anchor is raised. However, if the anchor is snagged, by moving the boat upwind or uptide of the anchor, the tripping line can be used to pull the anchor in a different direction to that possible with the main anchor rode. This often successfully frees a snagged anchor. A tripping line is well worth the effort unless you are absolutely sure that the bottom will be clear of obstructions.

Except in very small craft such as dinghies, never anchor without a length of chain between the anchor and the warp. Not only does the weight of the chain increase the holding capacity of the anchor, but it will survive obstacles such as rock, and sharp objects such as steel wreckage, which could well cut rope. In rough conditions a craft may snub violently at its anchor tackle, increasing chafe, the likelihood of breaking some gear, or breaking the anchor out of the bottom. The use of the chain reduces snubbing considerably.

Also, the weight of the chain between the boat and her anchor will cause it to hang in a curve. This is known as the catenary effect, and it greatly improves the motion of an anchored boat in choppy water. When a violent snub or jerk occurs, the chain is stretched taut. A similar effect can be created using a rope anchor rode and suspending a heavy weight halfway down the rope.

Opposite *Basic tools and spares (top); a DOT-approved life jacket (centre); a life harness (bottom).*

THE CATENARY EFFECT

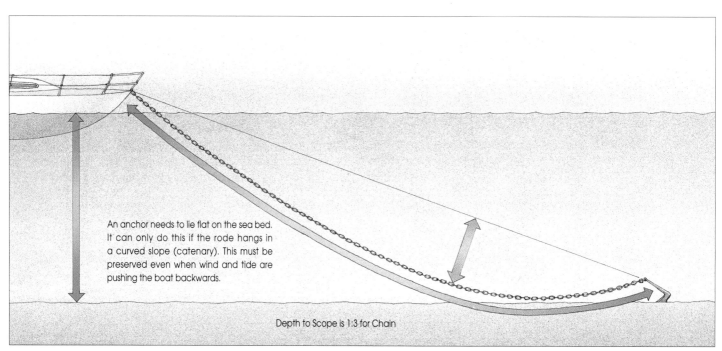

An anchor needs to lie flat on the sea bed. It can only do this if the rode hangs in a curved slope (catenary). This must be preserved even when wind and tide are pushing the boat backwards.

Depth to Scope is 1:3 for Chain

The Bitter End

The bitter end refers to the last section of the anchor chain or rope in the boat – it must be tied fast! Many are the anchors and tackle which have been lost overboard due to the bitter end simply being paid out over the side.

SPARES

Always bear in mind that a good seaman should be self-reliant and needs to be able to effect simple repairs and replacements at sea. A basic tool kit should be carried on all craft that go to sea. The normal selection of small tools such as screwdrivers, drills, pliers, mole wrench, spanners and hacksaw – with plenty of spare blades – should be included. A bolt cutter, capable of cutting the yacht's stays, is also a good idea. In the case of a dismasting it may be necessary to cut the wreckage adrift in a hurry. A multimeter and 12-volt soldering kit could also be included for simple electrical repairs.

Spares Kit

A list of spares for a moderate-sized cruiser-racer could look something like this:
- spare shackles
- spare thimbles and wire rope terminals
- spare winch handle or handles
- selection of stainless steel hose clamps
- spare kits of washers and diaphragms for bilge pumps and freshwater galley pumps
- spare bulbs for navigation, compass and cabin lights
- spare rope
- selection of blocks
- spare torches
- good supply of batteries for torches and other small electrical items such as a hand-held GPS
- spares for the stove, particularly burners
- engine spares, belts, fuel and oil filters, engine oil
- spare stainless steel pins and split pins
- variety of spare stainless steel bolts.

SAFETY GEAR

Safety gear requirements vary throughout the world, but many are based on those issued by the Offshore Racing Council (ORC) which governs the sport of offshore racing. Their requirements are very comprehensive. A few of the basics will be covered here.

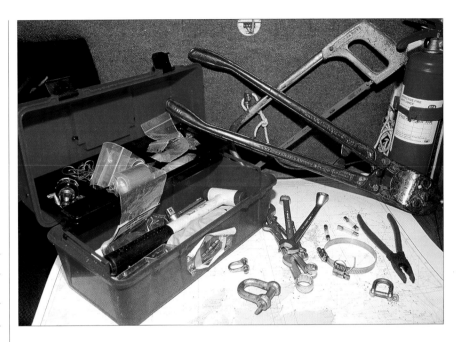

Life Jackets

It goes without saying that there should be a life jacket for every member of the crew. Some countries will insist that these be Department of Transport (DOT) approved. If you have a choice, select life jackets that can be worn comfortably while working the boat. Remember also that most buoyancy aids used in sailing dinghies do not qualify as life jackets. Life jackets should be equipped with a whistle and reflective strips, to enable them to be picked out at night.

Life Harnesses

Life harnesses need to be easy to put on, and should preferably have two stainless steel snap clips attached at different parts of the tether line. These hooks must be of a type that are difficult to open accidentally. When steering or working in a restricted area, the snap clip closest to the wearer should be used.

The boat must be checked over to ensure there is an adequate number of lifeline harness points of suitable strength. A strong attachment point needs to be provided near the main hatch to enable crewmen to clip on before leaving the safety of the cabin. A jackstay, running the full length of the craft on both sides, is necessary to ensure that the crew can move from cockpit to foredeck without having to reclip the harness. Do not be afraid to use harnesses if conditions look difficult, and always wear them at night.

Above *Life belts should always be unclipped (unlike the one illustrated here) when in position on the boat.*

Life Belts

Normally, two life belts are carried. These should be fitted with whistles and drogues, and for night sailing, with self-igniting lights. Most sailors prefer the horseshoe-shaped life belt, as you do not have to put your head underwater to get into it. The horseshoe type normally has a line to clip in place, bridging the gap created by the horseshoe and keeping the user encircled by the belt. On the boat, some people use this line to ensure that the life belt remains in its clips, or stowage position. This is not a good idea, as the clips will have to be undone before the belt can be thrown in an emergency.

Emergency Steering

The time could come when the steering system fails, and you need to be prepared for this eventuality. On tiller-steered boats, a spare tiller should be on board, predrilled and ready to fit to the rudderhead. On wheel-steered boats, an emergency tiller system that is easy to fit and operate should be available. In the case of the loss of the rudder, steering can usually be effected by bolting floorboards to a spinnaker pole, and lashing the pole to the pushpit. Purpose-made U-bolts and predrilled floor or bunkboards are a good idea. If all else fails, a reasonable course can usually be maintained in the open ocean by the use of sails, trimmed to suit the conditions.

Right *An electrical bilge pump.*
Below *A Dan buoy.*

Dan Buoys

Dan buoys are lightweight buoys that float upright in the water, fitted with a flag, or a light at night, to indicate the position of a man overboard. In the case of a person overboard in anything but calm conditions, throw the life belt and the Dan buoy simultaneously, if possible (some rules state that the life belt and Dan buoy should be attached). A person in the water is very difficult to see, and a crew member should be assigned to do nothing but watch that person while the yacht's crew prepare to pick him up.

Cockpit Drains

A very big problem with some yachts, particularly older ones, is inadequate cockpit drains. A cockpit holds a lot of water, and if a big sea fills it, it needs to drain rapidly. If the cockpit is drained via pipes and seacocks, these should be of large diameter. Many modern boats have cockpits which are partially open aft and drain automatically without the complication of pipes and seacocks; these work very well.

Seacocks

All through-hull fittings for items such as an engine-cooling water inlet, sink drains, etc., should be fitted with seacocks. Grease these regularly and make a habit of operating them all periodically to ensure they are free. A selection of softwood, conically-shaped plugs, suited to the diameter of the boat's seacocks, should be aboard at all times. In the event of damage to a seacock (heavy gear shifting for instance), a softwood plug can be hammered in from within the boat, stopping the flow of water. If your boat is to be left afloat unattended, close all seacocks before leaving her.

Bilge Pumps

Most safety rules call for two bilge pumps, one of which must be operable from below (inside the cabin). The majority of bilge pumps for small- to medium-sized boats are of the diaphragm type. They are excellent, resist clogging and move big volumes of water. Electrically operated pumps are also popular, but remember: in the case of failure of the vessel's power supply, they will not work.

Carry at least two heavy-duty (not necessarily metal) buckets. As the old joke goes, no pump is as efficient as a frightened man with a bucket!

INTERNATIONAL FLAG CODE SYSTEM

A (Alpha)   I have a diver down; keep clear and pass at low speed.

B (Bravo)   I am loading, unloading or carrying dangerous goods.

C (Charlie)   Yes; confirmation of preceding signal.

D (Delta)   Keep clear, I am manoeuvring with difficulty.

E (Echo)   I am altering course to starboard.

F (Foxtrot)   I am disabled, communicate with me.

G (Golf)   I require a pilot or (on fishing vessel) I am hauling in nets.

H (Hotel)   I have a pilot on board.

I (India)   I am altering course to port.

J (Juliet)   I am on fire and have dangerous cargo on board; keep clear.

K (Kilo)   I wish to communicate with you.

L (Lima)   You should stop your vessel immediately.

M (Mike)   My vessel is stopped and making no way through the water.

N (November)   No; the preceding signal should be read in the negative.

O (Oscar)   Man overboard.

P (Papa)   I am about to put to sea.

Q (Quebec)   My vessel is healthy and I request clearance to come ashore.

R (Romeo)   Single letter code R has no allocated meaning; see the IRPCS.

S (Sierra)   I am going astern under power.

T (Tango)   Keep clear, I am engaged in pair trawling.

U (Uniform)   You are running into danger.

V (Victor)   I require assistance.

W (Whisky)   I require medical assistance.

X (X-ray)   Stop carrying out your intentions and watch for my signals.

Y (Yankee)   I am dragging my anchor.

Z (Zulu)   I require a tug or (on a fishing vessel) I am shooting nets.

AP + CF (Answering pennant and code flag)
   The code flag is flown to show that the International Code is being used, and to acknowledge a message.

FS   First substitute.

SS   Second substitute.

TS   Third substitute.

0 (nought) to 9 Numericals.

Flags

Some basic flags must be carried. Flags N and C, from the International Code Flags, when flown N over C mean: 'I am in distress.' Flag V means: 'I need assistance.'

Flares

Red rockets and red hand flares are specified in most safety regulations. The hand flares can be visible for good distances at night, but the red rockets can be seen for many miles. Read the instructions for operating very carefully before setting out on a trip. A distress situation in the middle of a dark and windy night is no time to try and read the firing details on a rocket cartridge. White flares are also useful. They are not distress flares, but can be used to indicate

flare kit

red parachute rocket

red hand flare

THE USE OF DISTRESS SIGNALS

one's position if one is in danger of being run down by another vessel. Smoke floats are used as a daytime distress signal and should always be carried.

Sea Anchors

Sea anchors are controversial devices. Some swear by them in heavy weather, while others rate them as dangerous! The decision on whether to deploy one or not is the skipper's alone. Because of the controversy, the ORC recommends that they only be carried on the highest category races.

They have been developed tremendously in recent years and one of the popular types, particularly among multihull sailors, is the parachute sea anchor. It is large, dramatically reduces downwind drift and is claimed to calm the approaching waves to windward. These anchors are equipped with a tripping device to enable the parachute to be collapsed and the sea anchor retrieved.

Advocates of sea anchors say that they hold vessels steady during exceptional conditions, limit speed and therefore the danger of surfing at wave speed and pitchpoling. Sea anchors can be deployed over the bows or over the stern.

Often sailors who feel the need to slow down in bad weather, trail warps to do so. However, it takes many warps to equal the drag of a sea anchor. If you opt for the latter, both the anchor and its tether must be extremely strong. You need to also guard against chafe. Many users of sea anchors have reported that they can, and do, break free in extreme conditions. Therefore, if one of these anchors is part of your equipment, ensure that it is over specification.

A sea anchor is undoubtedly an asset in gale-force conditions, where progress to windward is impossible, and you are close to a lee shore. In this case, such an sea anchor could help to prevent drifting ashore. Modern boats have become continuously lighter, their downwind speed has increased tremendously and a means of slowing a boat down is therefore worth having. So in the windier parts of the world, both sea anchors and warps for trailing are a useful addition to the boat's equipment.

In an article in a British magazine in April 1998, Sir Robin Knox-Johnston (*see* page 108) came out strongly in favour of trailing warps. He pointed out that the rope, streamed in sufficient length in a bight (a loop that has both ends secured to the boat) from either side of the stern, succeeds in providing consid-

Left *An inflated life raft alongside a boat.*

erable drag. In addition, rope avoids the shock load a boat is subject to when the drag from the sea anchor comes on. Breakages of the painter (the rope used to make the anchor fast to the boat) or the holding points often occur at this time. Warps, coupled with a drogue, is the safest, and certainly least controversial answer to slowing down a modern, light boat in bad weather.

Emergency Position Indicating Radio Beacons (EPIRBs)

There are two basic types of EPIRBs. The first, the least effective, operates on the aircraft emergency frequencies of 121.5 MHz (civil aviation) and 246 MHz (military aviation). To be received, an aircraft needs to be flying fairly close to the area where the beacon has been activated.

A more effective EPIRB is the newer 406 MHz model. This operates via satellite, and coverage around the world is good. The licensing of a 406 MHz EPIRB is more stringent, but when triggered, its transmission records the name of the vessel, its registration details and the communications equipment carried. The satellite receiving the signal pinpoints the beacon's position. The information is relayed by the satellite to a ground station from where the information goes to the search and rescue authority nearest to the casualty. Rescue operations will then be mounted. Be warned that there are still parts of the world so remote from rescue services that it could be a long time, if ever, before contact is made with the craft in distress. The beacon will only transmit while it has sufficient battery power.

A 406 MHz EPIRB will also have a 121.5 MHz facility, as this is commonly used by search and rescue aircraft. If your boat is going to carry an EPIRB, the extra expense of the 406 MHz EPIRB does make sense.

Radio

VHF, SSB and ham radio have been covered in Chapter Eight. All can be used to transmit distress signals. Remember the limited range of VHF and

SAILING TERMS

- **Painter/tether**: rope at bow of a small boat, used to tie it up
- **Bight**: curve, or loop, in a rope
- **Drogue**: an object (e.g. a sea anchor) streamed from a boat to reduce its speed
- **Anchor rode**: the line, cable or chain connecting anchor to boat
- **Lying ahull** (hove-to): a boat lies with all its sails furled, usually to ride out a gale

also that the distress procedure is in the process of changing under Global Maritime Distress and Safety System (GMDSS).

Storm Covers

For craft with large window areas, storm covers should be stowed on board. There are many instances of a boat's windows being stove in, and a means of covering the aperture may be the difference between survival or not.

First-aid Kit

First aid has been discussed in Chapter Eight. The medical and first-aid kits should be considered part of the vessel's safety equipment.

Fire Extinguishers

Several fire extinguishers, strategically placed, should be carried. If, for instance, there is a fire in the main hatch area, it should be possible to enter the vessel via the forehatch and pick up a fire extinguisher in that area. Extinguishers should be serviced regularly. CO_2 extinguishers are not suitable because CO_2 is heavier than air and therefore sinks to the bottom of the boat; if the boat fills up with CO_2, the crew will not be able to breathe. These extinguishers are banned from marine use in most countries.

Left to right: *Foghorn, distress flares and fire extinguisher.*

Storm Sails

A heavy storm jib should definitely be carried. Some skippers argue that a heavily furled roller furler headsail acts as a suitable storm jib. But the more a headsail's area is reduced by furling, the worse it sets (it gets very baggy or full), and most roller furler headsails are not built strongly enough for exceptionally heavy winds. A storm trysail, while not essential, is a good investment. It can take the place of a mainsail if the main is badly damaged, apart from its primary function of being used in place of the mainsail in exceptionally bad conditions.

Spare Compass

A second compass, which could be a hand-held compass, is essential.

Second Set of Navigation Lights

Spare navigation lights should be carried. For craft fitted with running lights just above deck level, a tricolour qualifies as a spare. Alternatively, a separate set of lights, capable of being securely clipped onto the pushpit and pulpit and connected to a battery by jump leads, can be carried.

Foghorn

A foghorn, powered either by an aerosol can or by blowing with the mouth, must be carried.

Radar Reflector

The traditional aluminium radar reflector is still popular. There are many patent types which take up less space and are therefore easier to use. Do check the official claimed reflecting area to ensure that this is as effective as the standard type.

STORM TACTICS

No matter how carefully you plan a voyage and intend to avoid bad weather, the day will almost certainly come when you are forced to ride out some wild weather. The question is, how do you cope with it?

Most modern boats are capable of taking incredible punishment. They can go to windward in exceptionally strong winds, and provided sail is reduced and speed kept down, can be sailed safely downwind in very bad conditions.

If you are racing, you keep going until it becomes dangerous to carry on. When cruising, provided you do not have a lee shore under you, you have a choice. Why get wetter and more uncomfortable than you need to? Going downwind, sail can be reduced to a small jib, steering will remain relatively easy and good progress can be made. When conditions become difficult – and even under a small jib, regular surfing does occur – most yachts will continue happily downwind under 'bare poles' (without sails). Warps can be streamed, preferably in a bight, or a sea anchor deployed, when the skipper feels it would be safer to slow down. As mentioned earlier, modern hull shapes today, together with lighter weight, make boats sail fast downwind, and many yachts require a means of slowing down in exceptional weather. If bad weather occurs when your destination is up-wind, you can slow the boat down by reefing and setting a small headsail. If conditions worsen you can 'heave to' by sheeting the storm jib to windward, with a triple-reefed mainsail, or trysail set. Many yachts will lie very quietly like this at an angle of perhaps 45–50 degrees to the wind.

Some yachts will lie a-hull at much the same angle, with no sail set at all. It is important to know the characteristics of your own boat. As gales extend over a long period of time, the seas tend to continue building until it may not be prudent for your boat to lie in the 'hove to' or 'lying a-hull' position. With steep seas and breaking crests, damage could result, or a yacht could be knocked down or even rolled over. When

Left *A boat experiencing heavy wind conditions.*

Above *A yacht beating to windward in strong conditions.*

small craft and large vessels alike is when gales blow against an established current. Wind against waves created by current generates far bigger waves than those generated by winds of the same strength, or stronger, without the current. A good example is off the South African coast where the southwesterly gales blow against the Agulhas Current. Dangerous conditions result which, in this case, can be minimized by going inshore.

However, in most cases gales are better ridden out as far offshore as possible. Firstly, in deep water the waves produced by gales are much more regular and generally do less damage. Secondly, the more sea room one has, the less one has to worry about being driven ashore if a long period is spent lying a-hull, or hove to. Dangers, such as the Agulhas Current mentioned above, will be highlighted in the pilot books (*see* page 90).

Carry sufficient storm sails, even if they are never used. Also ensure heavy equipment such as stoves, batteries, tools and the like cannot break loose in a knockdown, or in the unlikely event of a roll over.

Ocean-going yachts are incredibly safe. Most will easily survive the type of weather described above. However, crews must be prepared for bad weather and have plans in place for coping with it. There is no one safe method to weather storms: each sailor has different ideas, all of which have probably worked for them.

MAN OVERBOARD

Losing someone overboard is something that should be avoided at all costs. In bad weather, harnesses should be worn. Even in good weather, the dangers of falling overboard should be emphasized and crew members and passengers should be conscious of this possibility at all times (*see* also page 51).

As a skipper, you must realize that in spite of all precautions, losing a person overboard could easily happen. As with so many things in sailing, there is no one way to recover a person overboard. It depends on the weather conditions, the type of boat and its handling characteristics and whether you are beating to windward, running or reaching. Another factor is whether the boat is under plain (normal) sail or has a spinnaker set.

Practise picking up a person overboard by having someone throw out a fender or life belt, and work out the quickest and best way of recovering it. Note,

yachts are caught in breaking waves, they are often swept along at the speed of the breaking crest and this can be extremely dangerous, particularly if the boat is rolled so far that the mast (or masts) dips in. Sea anchors or drogues can be an aid in these conditions by helping to prevent a craft travelling at the speed of the breaking wave, and can also help flatten the approaching seas. Many feel that the safest way to treat extreme conditions as described here is to run downwind, preferably using one of the methods of slowing down.

Certain parts of the world are renowned for bad weather at certain times, and one of the major causes of waves that break and cause damage to too, that once the person in the water has been reached, he or she has to be turned backwards and pulled aboard. This can be quite difficult with high freeboard boats. Many modern designs have sugar scoop sterns which make recovery somewhat easier – although not in high seas; the stern can crash down on the person in the water. Several devices have been invented for winching the person aboard.

When someone does go overboard, the life belt and Dan buoy must be thrown immediately. If they are connected, as some rules specify, you must ensure that they can both be released simultaneously. Even at a speed of some six knots, a vessel is travelling at about 10ft (3m) a second. In the time taken to realize the problem and deploy the gear, the vessel could be 100ft (30m) from the swimmer.

There are too many different methods of man overboard recovery to discuss each one in detail here, but some of the more common ones are described below:

Reach and Return on the Reciprocal Bearing

On losing a crew member overboard, put the yacht onto a reach, read the compass heading, go about or gybe, reach back on the reciprocal bearing and you should pass quite close to the swimmer. If spinnakers have to be struck and the boat cannot immediately be turned, gear can be thrown overboard at regular intervals to mark a track back to the person overboard.

Quick Stop Manoeuvre

Here the boat is stopped immediately, usually by tacking and heaving to, and halts close to the person overboard. The boat is rapidly sorted out, spinnakers dropped, and the person picked up. This is an excellent manoeuvre, but not suitable for a racing boat surfing downwind under spinnaker. A sudden luff would result in a broach and a knockdown which would have to be sorted out before the recovery exercise could begin.

Approaching the Man Overboard

The best approach is normally to have the swimmer on the boat's leeward side. The boat can be luffed up and brought to a near stop as the person is reached, making recovery easier. The reason for the leeward side generally being the easiest to get the

person aboard is, with the heeling angle of the boat, the deck would usually be fairly close to the water.

Auxiliary Engine

The engine may well be used in some circumstances. If it is employed, bear in mind that the propeller can severely injure a person in the water. Ensure that the engine is put into neutral as the swimmer is approached. It is recommended that, even if you are going to be picking up the man under sail, the engine is started and left running in neutral in case it is needed.

Push Buttons

Many electronic navigation devices such as GPS's have a button which can be pushed to fix the position of a person overboard. If you have such equipment, familiarize yourself with it and have a crew member activate it immediately. It will assist in finding the person overboard, particularly in bad weather. Not many people do fall overboard, but it is a risk which must be taken seriously.

Below *A crew member preparing to throw a float aid to a man who has fallen overboard.*

ALL-WEATHER SAILING GEAR

Recent progress made in clothing materials, particularly by the manufacturer Gore-Tex (leaders in breathable fabrics) has resulted in modern, lightweight, multilayered clothing that offers waterproofing qualities and heightened insulation from the cold. Layers comprising polyester wicking fibres for absorption of perspiration, a breathable intermediate shell that allows moisture to pass through into the atmosphere, and an outer waterproof nylon/neoprene lining (also breathable) protect sailors today from serious wind chill factors in the foulest weather.

Ocean jacket – for offshore and ocean racing in variable climates. Has a collar-hood attachment, and double cuffs prevent water and moisture from entering.

Salopettes – keeps trunk and legs warm without inhibiting arm movement. Elasticated shoulders, knee and seat patches protect vulnerable areas.

Trousers – reinforced knees and seat provide extra waterproof protection. Velcro straps at ankles ensure snug fit over boots.

Smock – in breathable waterproof nylon. Suitable for racing and cruising in coastal and inshore waters. Neoprene neck and wrist seals, and adjustable waistband ensure snug fit.

Leather gloves – come with long or short (i.e. cut-off fingers). These are for small boats, and have durable, padded palms that grip well. Offshore leather gloves have water-resistant fabric on the back, adjustable wrist straps and removable thermal liners.

Rubber boots – nonslip for wet conditions. Longer or shorter leg lengths available.

Opposite *Crew* *foul weather gear* *heavy conditions.*

CHAPTER TEN

HEALTH

MEDICAL ASPECTS

Accidents and problems do not only occur on seagoing boats, and all who use the water should be aware that problems can occur on any sort of marine outing. Sailors should therefore have some idea of how to deal with them, and a first-aid course is always a good step to take.

PRIORITIES

In the case of a boating accident occurring, the best emergency treatment sometimes is to do nothing, except minimize the danger to the patient, keep him or her out of harm's way, and attend to the safe running of the boat. Overreaction to a casualty could result in an accident to the boat such as capsizing (in a dinghy) or running aground, which will not only delay getting the casualty treatment, but could endanger the rest of the crew as well. The emphasis should be:

- protect the casualty from further danger
- protect other crew members and yourself
- ensure that the boat is safe
- send promptly for qualified help if available
- promote the recovery of the casualty if this is within the scope of knowledge among those on board the boat.

Top *First-aid kit.*

ASSESSING A CASUALTY

One of the first steps when you are dealing with an injured person is to ascertain the extent of the damage. Is the patient conscious or not? If he or she is, you will probably be able to gauge at least some indication of the problem. If the patient is not conscious, the most important question is: is the person able to breathe freely?

A rescue operation in progress.

The following check list is useful: Airway, Breathing, Circulation (ABC).

- *Airway*

  If the casualty is unconscious, check that the airway is clear. Noisy breathing indicates a blocked airway. Remove any obvious obstruction (dentures, for instance).

Tilt the head back by gently lifting the chin which will clear the tongue from the back of the throat and open the airway.

- *Breathing*

  Place your ear near the victim's mouth. If he or she is breathing you should be able to hear, or feel, a breath on your cheek. Is the abdomen rising and falling?

- *Circulation*

  Feel for the victim's pulse by placing your fingertips on the neck (just behind the Adam's apple in the case of a male), in the gap between the windpipe and the muscle alongside it.

If the ABC check shows a problem with breathing or circulation, the victim needs mouth-to-mouth resuscitation and also chest compression (cardiopulmonary resuscitation, or CPR, *see* page 155) until help arrives.

SPINAL INJURY

Never move a patient with any suspected spinal injury, except as an absolute last resort. Quick indicators of possible spinal injury are: the nature of the

Below *A casualty just recovered from the water receives attention from a fellow crew member.*

accident, the position in which the victim is lying, and the lack of sensation or movement in limbs. If a victim with suspected spinal injury has to be moved, use three or four people acting together (if they are available); move the head and trunk together, all the while keeping the head well supported. Avoid any rotation, or bending, of the spine.

The victim can be rolled onto a board (the yacht's floorboards, for example) if necessary. If the accident occurs ashore, a victim with a suspected spinal injury is often best left until competent people arrive (this is unlikely to be possible at sea).

NEAR DROWNING

With sailing casualties, capsizes in dinghies or a man overboard situation in larger boats, there is always a danger of liquid getting into the victim's lungs. In cold water, liquid can be drawn into the lungs when the victim gasps from the shock of falling into the water. Often only a small amount of liquid enters the lungs, but a throat spasm prevents the victim from breathing properly.

Another common cause of near drowning is when muscle co-ordination is lost in cold water, and the victim sinks, inhaling water.

A casualty recovered from the water who is not breathing should be given mouth-to-mouth resuscitation. If there is no pulse, CPR should be given. Be careful, however, for if hypothermia has been a factor, the pulse might be weak and difficult to find. Do not give CPR if there is a faint pulse, as heart damage could result.

Once treatment has been given, all near-drowning patients should be treated as suffering from hypothermia (*see* page 155).

It is most important, if the craft is able to return to port, that near-drowning patients are hospitalized for observation, no matter how normal they appear to be. Complications can and do arise from fluid retained in the lungs.

THE BODY CHECK

If the victim is conscious, and there are no problems with the ABC check, continue working down the length of the body, looking for any injuries. Keep talking to the casualty, even if he or she appears to be unconscious. Explain exactly what you are doing and reassure the patient. Remember, an obvious injury may not be the life-threatening one.

Head Start at the head. Look for obvious injury and check for blood or fluid coming from ears and nose which might indicate damage inside the skull. Feel if the skin is hot, cold, clammy or dry. These could suggest heatstroke, hypothermia, and/or shock. Is breathing fast, slow, deep or shallow? Check eyes for damage.

Neck Move down to the neck. Feel for any obvious injury or dampness from bleeding.

Trunk Work down both sides of the trunk. Press in the ribs carefully to see if there is a reaction by the victim, indicating a chest or rib injury. Feel under the back for obvious injury, deformity or bleeding.

Limbs Work along the arms and then legs. Feel for any swelling or bleeding, or unusual limb position. See if the casualty can move his or her arms, fingers and toes. If the injured person cannot, ask where the difficulty lies.

Diagnosis The body check only takes a few minutes, but could save a life if you are within reach of help or, if at sea, have a suitable radio. The casualty will be more likely to receive the correct treatment or be given the best advice.

THE RECOVERY POSITION

Once initial checks have been completed, the victim should be placed on his/her side in the recovery position (unless suffering from spinal injury), to prevent him or her from choking on vomit or ingesting acids produced by the stomach.

If the casualty is gently rolled onto his/her left side (with your hand supporting the person's left cheek), the head should rest on the left arm, which has been crooked with the palm behind the head, facing upwards. The right arm is flexed to 90 degrees, with the forearm placed flat on the ground, while the right knee is brought over the left leg and also flexed to 90 degrees.Once in this position, the patient should be wedged to hold it. The casualty will now be in the correct recovery position.

ATTENDING TO SPECIFIC INJURIES

Know your location. If possible, call for help. In coastal areas help can be summoned by telephone if you can get ashore; often a cell phone is within range of a network; or use a VHF radio. At sea on a passage, SSB radio and communication via satellite can be used by yachts carrying the necessary

MOUTH-TO-MOUTH RESUSCITATION

Gently tilt head back and lift chin to open airway. Ensure that obstructions in the mouth are not restricting breathing process.

Pinch patient's nostrils closed, take a deep breath and place your mouth firmly over that of the patient.

Exhale deeply into patient's mouth for two seconds and check to see whether chest rises. If it doesn't, recheck that airway is fully opened.

As patient's chest falls, breathe in again deeply and repeat process. Check pulse to see whether heart is beating. If there is a heart beat, continue breathing into patient's mouth every five seconds until patient's breathing returns to normal. At this point, place patient in the recovery position.

equipment. Once you have asked for help, you can then attend to the patient's specific injuries.

Bleeding

Blood loss must be attended to rapidly. There is not a great deal that can be done about internal bleeding, which may manifest itself by bruising, discoloration and/or bleeding from body openings, except to treat for shock (see below), which will almost certainly accompany such bleeding.

External bleeding is easier to treat. Elevation and direct pressure are the two main remedying applications. Elevating the wound will help slow the flow of blood. Direct pressure can be applied with anything available, even a dirty rag, though this should be used only as a very last resort, because of the danger of infection. The priority at this stage is stopping the bleeding, not hygiene.

Apply a dressing to the wound as soon as possible, but do not bind the wound too tightly, otherwise blood flow could be stopped. If blood comes through the dressing, put another one on top – do not try and remove the first dressing.

A tourniquet should only be applied to a limb if the damage is so severe that amputation is likely. Tourniquets will stop blood flow, but if left on for any length of time, will cause gangrene to set in.

Burns

Contrary to some opinions in the past, the only first-aid treatment for burns is immersing the affected area in cold, fresh water. Water is scarce while making a passage, but must be used in the case of severe burns. Remove anything covering the burn (clothing, watches, etc.). Ten minutes is the minimum immersion time, more for a severe burn. Prompt treatment will have dramatically beneficial effects.

Do not apply lotions, ointments or creams to any burn. If the skin is not broken, leave the burn open to the air. If it is blistered or broken, use a light dressing made of nonfluffy material. Plastic film makes an ideal burn dressing.

Scalds caused by hot liquids – common on seagoing yachts – should be treated in the same way. Treat burn victims for shock (see right).

Sunburn

Sunburn should be avoided at all costs, especially in tropical and subtropical areas where the sun is exceptionally strong. Use high-factor, waterproof sun blocks. Sun damage may cause skin cancer and rodent ulcers many years later. Make sure you wear clothes that keep the skin covered, and always wear a hat to protect your head and face.

Eye Protection

Only use good quality sunglasses which filter out most of the harmful ultraviolet rays, to protect the eyes from the harsh glare of the sun. Attach sunglasses to a cord hung around the neck to prevent them from falling overboard if they get knocked off.

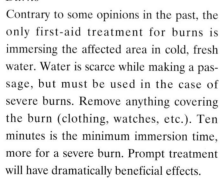

Heat Exhaustion

This problem, prevalent in the tropics and subtropics, often results from dehydration and salt loss. Cruising sailors in hotter climates tend to take salt tablets every day to counteract this.

To treat heat exhaustion, the patient should lie down and legs should be raised. A salt solution should also be ingested; two teaspoons of salt to 1 litre (2pt) of water makes a suitable solution.

Shock

With anything more than a minor injury or accident, it can be assumed the patient will have suffered some degree of shock.

Initial signs of shock are:
- a rapid pulse
- pale, grey skin (a fingernail or earlobe, if pressed, does not regain its normal colour immediately)
- unnatural sweating, and cold, clammy skin.

As shock develops, patients may become weak, giddy and nauseous. Vomiting may also occur and breathing becomes rapid and shallow.

The treatment for shock is simple and effective. Firstly, treat the obvious cause of the shock, such as bleeding or burns. Lie the casualty down, keep the head low and raise the feet to aid blood supply to the brain. Loosen tight clothing, belts or equipment. Keep the casualty warm and insulated. It is also important to keep him or her reassured.

Do not allow the casualty to eat, drink, smoke or move about. If he or she is thirsty, the lips should be moistened with water.

Hypothermia

Exposure, as hypothermia is commonly known, is caused by a combination of wet and cold. Bad diet, tiredness, inadequate clothing, and physical and mental attitude can all be contributory factors. Before sailing, or during a passage, ensure that:

- the weather is favourable when starting out
- all the crew members are correctly clothed and equipped
- everyone is properly fed and adequate rations are on board
- the planned trip is well within the capabilities of the crew
- everyone is in good health (no colds or 'flu).

In bad weather and wet conditions, keep talking to crew members on duty – hypothermia often creeps up unnoticed.

Signs of hypothermia include:

- shivering and cold, marble-like skin
- general apathy, confusion, irrational or drunken-like behaviour
- complaints of tiredness, coldness or cramp (particularly calf muscles) and blurred vision.

Treatment for hypothermia:

- shelter from the elements (get the victim out of the wind and the rain)
- provide insulation from above and below
- start gentle warming (another person in the sleeping bag with the casualty is a good method)
- ask for help if possible.

Do not apply hot-water bottles, rub the skin or give any alcohol. Hot drinks such as soup or chocolate are fine. Boosting the morale of the patient plays an important role.

Fractures

In the case of minor fractures, fingers should be strapped to each other; a broken arm should be supported in a sling and strapped to the body; a broken leg can be immobilized by strapping it to the other leg (splints are not widely used these days). Fractures should be seen by a doctor as soon as possible.

Cuts and Wounds

On a cruising yacht, someone needs to be able to suture if necessary. However, with the aid of steri-strips and butterfly bandages, a comparatively large wound can be closed without stitching.

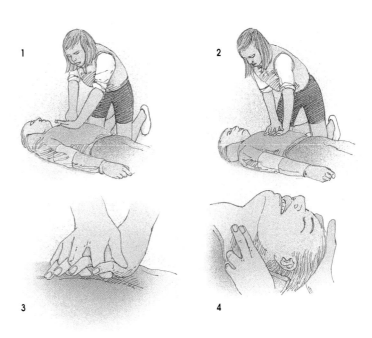

CARDIOPULMONARY RESUSCITATION (CPR)

MALARIA

Malaria is prevalent in some of the tropical and subtropical areas of the world. You should take prophylactics as a precaution; treatment should start some 10 days to two weeks before a trip – your pharmacist will be able to advise you when to start. Note that there are different strains of malaria which require different preventative medication. Ask your local doctor for advice.

SEA SICKNESS

An extremely common form of illness on the ocean, sea sickness in its worst form is completely debilitating and can result in dehydration. Every first-aid kit should carry drugs (there are many available) to alleviate or cure this illness. In extreme cases, suppositories are usually effective. Some medications can induce drowsiness.

COMMON PROBLEMS

In addition to dehydration and lack of salt, a common ailment, particularly in the tropics, is skin fungus infection for which antifungal creams can be applied. Cuts can become infected and must be kept dry to prevent infections from developing further, as these may take a long time to heal. Antibiotics should be carried by those making long passages.

Above *To carry out CPR, take the following steps:*
Step 1 *Place heel of one hand (lengthwise) two finger-points above where rib cage meets breastbone.*
Step 2 *With straight arms, place heel of other hand over first one, interlocking fingers.*
Step 3 *Press down on lower half of breastbone, keeping arms straight, and release. Smoothly complete 15 compressions at three-second intervals.*
Step 4 *Alternate CPR with mouth-to-mouth ventilation (two breaths). Check pulse every three minutes.*

GLOSSARY

Aft At, towards, or near the stern of a vessel. Also, aftermost e.g. aftermost mast (see also Forward).

A-hull A sailboat is lying a-hull when it is lying with all sails furled; associated with tactics for riding out gales.

Anchor rode The anchor line, rope or cable connecting the anchor to the vessel.

Apparent wind The direction of the wind over the deck of a vessel. It is resultant of the speed and direction of the true wind plus the speed and direction of the boat (see also True wind).

Astern Behind the vessel. To go astern means to reverse.

Back To push a sail out, or sheet it so that the wind catches it from the other side (the sail is then backed).

Backstay A stay which normally goes from the masthead to the stern of a vessel.

Ballast Weight, the purpose of which is to increase stability. The weight in a keel is considered to be ballast.

Battens Thin strips of wood, plastic or glass-reinforced plastic, used to help with sail shape and/or extend the roach.

Beam The width of a boat, normally at its point of maximum breadth.

Beam reach Reaching with the true wind at right angles to the centreline.

Bear away Alter course away from the wind.

Bear down To approach a sailboat from upwind.

Bearing The direction of an object expressed in degrees related to a compass. Bearings can be given as true or magnetic.

Beating Sailing to windward (upwind), by repeated tacking.

Belay To secure a rope to a cleat or belaying pin. Also an instruction meaning 'stop'.

Berth A bunk or a mooring.

Bight The section of a rope, usually in the form of a curve or loop, between its two ends. Also an indentation in a coastline or the body of

water within that indentation.

Bilge The bottom of the boat; also the water that collects there (bilge water).

Bitter end The end of a warp or chain; often used in connection with the anchor rode. If the bitter end is not made fast, the anchor and its rode can be lost.

Block Describes the combination of a revolving pulley and its casing. A block and tackle is a hoisting device where a rope/chain is passed around a pair of blocks (see also Tackle).

Boom A spar, or pole. The foot of the mainsail is normally attached to a boom. Spinnakers also require booms to set properly.

Boom preventer A rope or tackle used to steady the boom. It assists in preventing accidental gybes.

Boom vang Also known as a kicking strap, a tackle or line attached to the boom which prevents it from riding up when the mainsheet is eased and the vessel heads downwind.

Bosun's chair A seat made of strong fabric or wood, to hoist a person up the mast in safety.

Bow The forward section of a vessel.

Bowsprit A spar extending forward from the bow of a vessel; normally used for setting headsails.

Broach To slew in a following sea or wind. The vessel rounds up violently and, in the case of a sailboat, can be heeled over to an alarming angle.

Broad reach A point of sail between a reach and a run.

Bulkhead A partition, normally running across (widthwise) the vessel. It can be structural and also watertight.

Bulwark The raised solid surface around the perimeter of the deck.

Burgee A triangular flag, often representing the yacht club to which the vessel belongs.

Cable An anchor chain, rope or rode. Also one-tenth of a nautical mile.

Camber The curved shape designed into a sail. Also the curve of a deck,

normally upwards from the gunwale towards the centreline.

Capstan A winch or windlass with a vertical drum, used for hauling in the anchor cable.

Centreboard A board which pivots downwards from a centreboard case; main use is to prevent a sailboat making leeway (see also Daggerboard, Leeboards and Keel).

Chainplates The metal (often stainless steel) plates bolted to the hull or parts of the hull structure to which shrouds and stays are attached.

Chart datum The water level, usually the level of the lowest tide, from which all the depths shown on a chart are measured.

Chord A curved line, parallel to the foot of the sail, joining the leech and luff. If an imaginary straight line is drawn between the luff and the leech, depth of the chord can be measured between the two.

Cleat A metal, wooden or plastic device with two arms around which rope can be made fast.

Clew The lower aft corner of a fore-and-aft sail where the leech meets the foot. (See also Tack.)

Close-hauled A sailing vessel is close-hauled when sailing as close to the wind as possible.

Cockpit A well, normally towards the stern of a sailing vessel. The helmsman steers from the cockpit while the crew use it for working the vessel and trimming sails.

Companionway The main entrance into a seagoing sailboat, usually via a hatch leading to a ladder.

Cringle An eye or loop built into a sail. Cringles are used at the clew and tack, at reef points, and to secure slides and hanks to the luff of sails.

Cunningham cringle An eye, or cringle, in the luff of a sail above the tack. The luff is hauled tight by the Cunningham tackle, making the sail flatter.

Daggerboard Similar to a centreboard, except that a daggerboard

does not pivot – it slides down a purpose-made trunk or case. It is used primarily to prevent leeway (see also Centreboard, Keel and Leeboards).

Dead Reckoning Known as DR, it is a method of navigating by meticulously recording the course sailed, leeway, speed, current drift and other factors at regular intervals, starting from a known position (see also Observed Position).

Deck The deck partially or completely covers the interior of a boat.

Dead run A point of sailing where a vessel is running exactly with the wind, i.e. the wind is blowing down the vessel's centreline.

Displacement The displacement of a vessel is the weight of the water it displaces when floating normally. The weight of the displaced water equals the weight of the boat.

Downhaul A rope used to haul down a sail such as a spinnaker, the downhaul in the case of the spinnaker operating via the spinnaker boom.

Downwind A point of sailing with the wind aft of the beam; term is used for broad reaching or running.

Draft (Draught) The depth of a vessel under the water, measured from the waterline to the lowest point of the keel.

Drogue An object streamed from a boat to reduce its speed; a sea anchor is considered a drogue.

Ease To let out a line, sheet or anchor cable gradually.

Ebb tide The tide is ebbing when it flows back from high to low water (see also Flood tide).

Ensign A flag flown by a vessel to indicate its nationality.

Fairlead A ring, fitting or channel to guide a rope in the right direction, reducing chafing to a minimum.

Fairway A channel, often the main shipping channel, in restricted waters.

Fall The part of a rope, leading from a block and tackle, which is hauled on.

Fathom A unit of measure, normally used with regard to water depth. 1 fathom = 6ft (1.8m).

Fin keel A keel which is not an integral part of a sailing vessel's hull shape, but a separate appendage. Fin keels are often bolted on.

Fix A fix is the vessel's position taken by obtaining accurate bearings by compass, sextant or other means.

Flood tide The tide is flooding when it rises from low to high (see also Ebb tide).

Flukes The pointed parts of an anchor which dig into a lake- or seabed.

Foot The lower, or bottom, edge of a sail.

Foresail A triangular sail, such as a jib, set forward of the mast. Also known as a headsail.

Forward ('forrard') Towards the bow of a vessel.

Freeboard The distance between the gunwale at deck level and the water.

Free wind Wind which is aft of the beam, e.g. running free.

Furl To roll a sail and fasten it with ties to the boom, or to furl a headsail with roller furling gear.

Gaff An angled spar, similar to a boom, which supports the head of a gaff sail.

Galley The kitchen of a vessel.

Gaskets Lengths of line or webbing used to tie a stowed sail to the boom. Also known as ties.

Genoa A large headsail which extends well aft of the mainmast.

Gimbals A swivelling device which enables a galley stove or compass card to remain level.

Go about To turn a sailing vessel through the head-to-wind position in order to change tacks.

Gooseneck A fitting which allows movement in all directions from a fixed point, usually used to attach the boom to the mast.

Goosewing To sail downwind with the mainsail on one side and the headsail (usually poled out) on the other.

Gunwale ('gunnel') The top edge of the hull where, in the case of a decked vessel, the hull meets the deck.

Guy A rope or wire used to control a spar; often a spinnaker guy acting on the spinnaker boom.

Gybe To change course by turning the stern through the wind. A fore-and-aft sail will be moved from the left side of the boat to the right, or vice versa.

Halyard A rope or wire (or combination of rope and wire) used to hoist sails.

Hanks Specially designed clips which attach sails to stays.

Harden up Sail closer to the wind.

Heading The compass direction in which the vessel is pointed.

Headsail See Foresail.

Heads The vessel's toilet(s).

Head-to-wind The vessel is pointed directly into the wind.

Heave to To virtually stop the boat, normally by sheeting a headsail to windward.

Heel To lean over or list. The bottom of the mast is known as the heel, as is the aft of the keel.

Helm The wheel or the tiller by which a vessel is steered.

Helmsman The person steering a vessel.

Hiking out Helping to keep a sailboat on a more even keel by leaning out, using toe straps to hold one's feet (see also Trapeze).

Hitch A knot which can be undone rapidly by pulling against the direction of strain which is holding it. To hitch is also to tie a rope to a spar or stay.

Holding ground The ground into which an anchor can dig.

Hounds The part of the mast to which stays and shrouds are attached.

Hull The main body of the boat, i.e. bottom and sides.

Inboard Situated within the hull; towards the centreline.

In irons A sailing vessel is 'in irons' when it is pointing directly into the wind and has lost its momentum.

Inshore Close to, or towards, the shore.

Isobars Lines on a weather map which join areas of equal barometric pressure.

Jam cleat A cleat into which a rope can be secured by jamming. It may have no moving parts, or it may be operated by cams (rotating mechanical devices).

Jib A triangular sail attached to the forestay (see also Foresail).

Jury rig A temporary arrangement to replace damaged rigging and/or spars.

Keel An appendage that is positioned to aid the righting of a sailboat and prevent leeway (see also Centreboard, Daggerboard and Leeboards).

Kicking strap See Boom vang.

Knot One knot equals a speed of one nautical mile per hour.

Lanyard A short length of light line or rope that is useful for attaching items such as a torch to one's wrist or a bucket to the boat so that they will not be lost overboard.

Lee The sheltered area downwind (away from the direction from which the wind is blowing) of a vessel.

Leeboards Boards (normally they will pivot) fixed vertically to the sides of a sailing vessel to prevent leeway (see also Centreboard, Daggerboard and Keel).

Leech The rear (aft) edge of a fore-and-aft sail. A symmetrical spinnaker has two leeches.

Leeward ('loo'ard') Toward the lee, or sheltered, side; the direction towards which the wind is blowing (see also Windward).

Leeway The sideways drift of a vessel caused by the wind. Also the distance between the course steered and the course achieved.

Lifeline A safety line fitted around the deck or fore and aft.

Lift A rope or wire supporting a spar (see also Topping lift).

Log An instrument used to measure the boat's speed through the water and distance travelled. Also short for logbook.

Luff The forward, or leading, edge of a sail. To luff up is to head a boat closer into the wind.

Mainsail The principal sail of a sailboat; always aft in a fore-and-aft rigged boat.

Mainsheet The rope, normally run through a series of blocks, that controls the trim of the mainsail.

Mark A fixed feature, either afloat or ashore, used as a guide for navigation.

Mast A vertical pole (spar) on a sailboat used for setting sails.

Masthead The topmost section of a mast.

Masthead rig A rig where the headsail and its stay extend from the bow to the masthead, e.g. a masthead sloop, yawl, etc.

Mast step The fitting, or structure, into which the heel of the mast fits.

Mercator projection A type of map projection that depicts a section of the earth's surface as flat; lines of latitude run parallel to each other, as do lines of longitude, crossing at right angles to form a perfect rectangular grid.

Meridian An imaginary circle drawn around the earth, passing through the north and south poles. All lines of longitude are meridians.

Millibar A unit of barometric pressure used in measuring atmospheric pressure: 1000 millibars = 1 bar.

Mizzen mast The mast closest to the stern on a vessel with two or more masts, except on a two-masted schooner where the aftermast is longer and is known as the mainmast. A mizzen is also the sail set on the mizzen mast.

Narrows A narrow channel.

Nautical almanac A book, published annually, containing navigational and astronomical data. It enables a mariner to fix his position when used in conjunction with sextant angles and navigation tables.

Nautical mile A unit of length used in navigation, equal to 6076ft (1852m). Also equal to one minute of latitude, the 60th part of one degree of latitude.

No go zone The area which defines the limits of a boat's ability to sail without tacking (as a result of wind direction impeding forward progress).

Observed position A vessel's position obtained by direct observation of features on a chart, or by observation of celestial bodies by sextant (see also Dead reckoning).

Offshore At some distance from the shore.

Offwind Any point of sailing away from the wind.

One design A sailboat built to comply with a strict set of rules. The purpose is to produce a fleet of boats with identical speeds.

Onshore On, or towards, the land, e.g. an onshore breeze.

Outhaul A rope used to tighten the foot of a sail by hauling its clew out along the boom.

Overfall A rough stretch of water, often caused by currents flowing over an underwater object.

Painter A line attached to the bow of a small boat, used to tow it or tie it up.

Pilot A person qualified to navigate a vessel into or out of harbours or rivers. Normally merchant ships require pilots in order to enter and leave port.

Pilotage Navigating a vessel through inshore waters.

Plot To mark a boat's position on a chart.

Points of sailing A series of terms (e.g. beating, reaching, running, etc.) describing the angle between a sailboat and wind direction.

Pontoon A floating platform to which a boat may be secured, or the floats supporting such a platform.

Port The left-hand side of a vessel when facing the bow. Also a harbour.

Port tack A sailing vessel is said to be on port tack when the wind comes over her port, or left side (see also Starboard tack).

Position line A line, usually drawn on a chart, along which the vessel's position is located.

Preventer A line, or tackle, which prevents excess movement of a mast or boom; it is often used on the boom as a gybe preventer.

Prow The front section of a vessel including the bow.

Pulpit A guardrail at the bow of a boat, usually a structure built of stainless steel or aluminium tubing.

Pushpit A guardrail at the stern of a boat, usually a structure built of stainless steel or aluminium tubing.

Quarter That area of a boat between the beam and the stern.

Race A rapid current, often caused by restricting the flow of water through a narrow channel.

Rating A rating is normally derived from a mathematical formula which attempts to rate a sailboat's speed potential, enabling it to race with other craft on an equitable handicap basis.

Ratlines Lines lashed between adjacent stays to form steps, or rungs.

Reach A point of sailing with the wind approximately at right angles to the boat.

Reef To reduce the size (area) of a sail for operation in heavy weather.

Reef points Reinforced areas of the sail through which line can be reeved to contain the reefed portion of the sail. The line can be permanently attached to the sail.

Reeve To pass a rope through a block, or an eye of a narrow opening.

Rig The arrangement of mast, spars and sails carried by a sailing vessel, e.g. sloop rig.

Rigging The collective term for the standing and running rigging supporting the spars and operating the sails.

Roach The curved part of the trailing edge (leech/rear) of a sail which extends outwards of an imaginary straight line between the head and clew of the sail.

Rode See Anchor rode.

Rudder A movable underwater foil, normally at or towards the stern, used for steering.

Run To sail with the wind directly behind the centreline of the boat.

Running rigging The sheets and halyards which control the raising, lowering and set of the sails (see also Standing rigging).

Safety harness A harness worn by crew members in bad weather. It is attached to the boat by a stout line and clip.

Samson post A vertical wooden or metal post on the boat to which ropes or cables may be secured.

Sand bar A bar is an underwater ridge of sand or mud. Many harbour entrances and river mouths have bars.

Seacock A below-waterline valve, which can be closed, usually placed as a safety device on through-the-hull fittings. It permits engine-cooling saltwater to enter the system. It also allows the pumping out of bilge water.

Shackle A U-shaped metal device, usually closed by a threaded pin, used for attaching blocks, fittings, etc., on the boat.

Shank The shaft of an anchor.

Sheave A pulley wheel.

Sheet The rope attached to the clew of a sail or, via a tackle, to the boom; it is used to control sail trim.

Shrouds Wires supporting the mast, fixed at deck level on either side of it (see also Stays and Standing rigging).

Slack tide The short period at high and low tide when there is no tidal movement (also, slack water).

Slides The mainsail can be secured to the mast by a number of slides, which run up a track of the mainmast.

Slip To let go or release, e.g. to slip a mooring line; also short for slipway or, in America, a marina berth.

Snatch block A block with a quick release device, allowing a rope to be inserted by opening the side of the block.

Spars A general term which collectively describes masts, booms, yards, etc. on sailing vessels.

Spinnaker A large, normally lightly constructed, full headsail for downwind use; usually multicoloured.

Spreaders Struts on either side of the mast, situated in pairs. They increase the spread of the shrouds and stays, improving the support for the mast. Also known as cross-trees.

Spring A mooring line led aft from the bow or forward from the stern. It stops a vessel moving forwards and backwards when moored.

Stanchions Upright posts, normally constructed of metal, that support guardrails and lifelines.

Standing rigging The shrouds and stays that support the mast/s (see also Running rigging).

Stand on To maintain a course. A right-of-way vessel is known as the stand-on vessel.

Starboard The right-hand side of a vessel when facing the bow.

Starboard tack A sailing vessel is said to be on starboard tack when the wind comes over her starboard, or right, side (see also Port tack).

Stays Wires attached to the mast to support it (see also Shrouds and Standing rigging).

Staysail A sail, normally smaller than the main headsail, attached to a stay forward of the mast.

Steerageway A vessel has steerageway when she is moving through the water fast enough to allow her to be steered.

Stern The aft section of a vessel.

Stock That part of the rudder to which the tiller is fitted.

Synoptic chart A weather map, showing isobars, fronts, lows and highs.

Tack The forward lower corner of a sail (see also Clew). Also, to turn a sailboat through the eye of the wind, i.e. to go from port tack to starboard tack and vice versa.

Tackle A rope-and-pulley system to provide gearing on such items as boom vangs or mainsheet.

Tangs The metal plates on the mast to which stays and shrouds are attached.

Telltales Small lengths of wool or spinnaker cloth sewn onto both sides of sails to indicate the airflow. Used to trim sails to best advantage.

Ties See Gaskets.

Tiller The wooden or metal bar attached to the rudder post or stock that enables the rudder to be turned.

Tiller extension A flexibly mounted extension on the tiller, allowing the helmsman to sit outboard of the centreline.

Toe straps Loops into which dinghy crew members can put their feet in order to assist hiking, or sitting out.

Topping lift A rope, wire or tackle supporting the end of the boom when the sail is lowered (see also Lift).

Track The course of a vessel. Also tracks for fittings, e.g. mainsheet or genoa track.

Training run A point of sailing between a broad reach and a dead run when the jib starts to collapse in the lee of the mainsail.

Transit Two items are in transit when, to the eye of the viewer, they are in line with one another. The term is used in pilotage.

Transom The flattish aft face of the stern of a boat.

Trapeze A wire (or wires) attached to a harness worn by the crew, and sometimes also the helmsman, of a dinghy to keep the boat on an even keel and maintain boat speed. The trapeze supports the weight of the crew member leaning out, normally on the windward side.

Traveller A fitting that slides on a track, enabling the sheeting angle of a sail to be adjusted.

Trim Boat trim is the fore-and-aft inclination of a boat. Crew weight forward will trim the bow down, and weight aft, the stern. To trim a sail is to set it for maximum efficiency.

True wind The speed and direction of the actual wind as it would be perceived if the vessel is not moving (see also Apparent wind).

Trysail A small, loose-footed, strongly made sail, used in place of a mainsail in very heavy weather.

Uphaul A rope or tackle used to lift a spar such as a spinnaker boom.

Upwind Sailing upwind means the vessel is going to windward. Upwind of a vessel means to windward of her (see also Windward).

Vang A rope used to support a gaff or spit (a type of spar); see also Boom vang.

Veer A clockwise shift in wind direction ('back' is anticlockwise).

Warp A rope used to moor or secure a vessel. To warp a vessel is to move it by hauling (winching) it with ropes.

Weather side The upwind, or windward, side of a boat (see also Lee side).

Whisker pole A short pole normally used on dinghies to pole out the jib to windward while on a run.

Winch A hand-operated or powered device for hauling in sheets or anchor cables.

Windward The direction from which the wind is blowing, or upwind; the windward, or weather, side of the boat (see also Upwind).

Yard A spar suspended from a mast, often transversely to the boat, to spread a square sail.

Yaw A motion pulling the bow to port or starboard as a vessel plunges through waves.

Yawl A two-masted sailing vessel with a short mizzen mast, normally stepped aft of the rudder post.

INDEX

Folios in italic text represent photographs